Sandy Williams—

Thanks for your kind words on the parts I sent to you previously

Ju Velli

Notes of Caring

Life's Lessons Learned

Jim Williams

Copyright © 2013 Jim Williams.

All rights reserved. No part of this book may be used or reproduced by any means, graphic, electronic, or mechanical, including photocopying, recording, taping or by any information storage retrieval system without the written permission of the publisher except in the case of brief quotations embodied in critical articles and reviews.

WestBow Press books may be ordered through booksellers or by contacting:

WestBow Press
A Division of Thomas Nelson
1663 Liberty Drive
Bloomington, IN 47403
www.westbowpress.com
1-(866) 928-1240

Because of the dynamic nature of the Internet, any web addresses or links contained in this book may have changed since publication and may no longer be valid. The views expressed in this work are solely those of the author and do not necessarily reflect the views of the publisher, and the publisher hereby disclaims any responsibility for them.

Any people depicted in stock imagery provided by Thinkstock are models, and such images are being used for illustrative purposes only.

Certain stock imagery © Thinkstock.

ISBN: 978-1-4908-0165-0 (sc)
ISBN: 978-1-4908-0166-7 (e)

Library of Congress Control Number: 2013912429

Printed in the United States of America.

WestBow Press rev. date: 7/23/2013

... <u>Walking On</u> ...

As I go through life, I notice the incredible work of grace that it has become. I am acutely aware that a great deal of my actions and reactions in human relations have everything to do with self image. How I think about myself determines:

1) What I dare to do in facing challenges,
2) Who I talk to and what I say,
3) How I think of other people. Thought life, in general

If someone really "takes a liking to me", a poor self-image will limit the esteem I hold him or her in. If I already know them to be esteemed highly publicly, then their high estimation of me lifts my self-esteem. The Bible is talking practical common sense when it says that we ought not to think of ourselves too highly, but so as to have a sound mind. It's a very core issue, rippling into the rest of our being significantly.

Tell me what you think, I'm just thinkin out loud.

<u>Hang In There!</u>

A little learning is a dangerous thing, it is said. A jury in California was presented with more information than was the general public, and out came a very unpopular verdict. We think we have more information than the public does, because we believe the bad things about ourselves that we may have heard for years. In the face of a bad self-image, our popularity among others is an unpopular thought. God has to work long and hard to turn this around. I am sixty one years old, and have never been able to take teasing well, because I always perceived it negatively. Some fellow missionaries of mine on a trip to Guatemala did not know it, but they were the first ever to make me feel loved by merciless teasing. Ask them what it was all about, but God showed me on that trip, and I finally believed it: Being teased was being loved. It took so many years for me to see myself as lovable.

It's still a struggle, but an awesome God has done it. He can do it for you, too. Just hang in there. He who began a good work ***will*** complete it!

Tell me what you think; I'm just thinkin' out loud.

Steppin out, and just out steppin

My mother, a pilot in past years, has a flying buddy in her women's pilots group who was scared to fly over water, so she just did it. She got out there and flew. My family would be out on the Mississippi River skiing and tanning, and along came Chris in the air flying a few hundred feet over the water. She just addressed her fear and conquered it.

I remember the mother of the character Velvet Brown in the movie "National Velvet". As a younger woman, she swam across the English Channel. She recalled to Velvet that she nearly drowned one time, but she later ended up swimming the sixteen miles to France.

Sometimes fear is a mirage, stretch of something we think we see, but sometimes a negative self-image, or other fear, tries to make it real for us. Once we dare to go forward, to step out, we keep stepping and find it's not there. What kind of mirage is keeping you from going after what you really want? Be careful, go slowly, but **go**! Pretty soon you'll see that steppin' out becomes just out steppin'. Try it!

Tell me what you think; I'm just thinkin' out loud.

Blessings, Train Stations, and Tea Bags

Once upon a time, in Memphis Tennessee, there were two kinds of train stations. One, the Union Station, was a station where the trains approached and departed from and to one direction. Down the street, at the other station, the Grand Central was another arrangement. Some of the tracks came and went from one direction, but others came and went from other directions. One famous train, the City of New Orleans, could approach and depart Memphis just like it did at the depots in small towns, from either direction.

Blessings are a bit like the two stations. Some just come to you and stop. Other blessings come to you, and, if you let them, go right through. As they pass, though, they take a bit of you with them. They take your smile, tone of voice, etc.

While I like both kinds of train stations and have no strong preference in that regard, I favor the kind of blessings that go through me.

Blessings have a resemblance to tea bags, too. Water never goes through a bag with being colored and flavored by the contents of the bag. What comes out of the bag depends on the contents of the bag, and it has reacted to the processes applied to it. It's sort of like the flavoring and coloring people have in their souls. As a result of the mixture of their attitude, their experiences, and their reactions to those experiences, they act and react in certain ways to opportunities. So does a tea bag when it steeps in hot water. The flavor you taste when you drink the tea is similar in nature to the "flavor" someone else experiences when you are a blessing to them.

So, tell me. What kind of tea bag are you? What is going to come out when you let a blessing flow through you?

Tell me what you think, I'm just thinking out loud!

Play Reveille!!

It is on the occasion of the passing of former U.S. President Richard Nixon that I write. He was more than a person; he was an era, larger than life. I suppose this summation comes from his having had such a major role in national and world history in the latter half of this century. I tend to take some comfort from the presence of such powerful people whose judgment I trust. This applies to leaders on local levels as well as national ones. When a pastor I like leaves town, I am sad and a little fearful that I won't be as comfy with the next guy in that place. It jars my world to experience such a change.

Richard Nixon was as large-scale a player as any president could ever be. He showed tremendous insight and fortitude in his dealings with other world leaders. He went to Russia, he went to China. He dared go to those places to try to reason with their leaders. How often I forget that every world leader is just a person. He or she is a very powerful person, but Romans 13:1 says that there is not a ruler on the earth that God did not put there and give power to. Nixon was a leader who recognized his position as a mission to be a peacemaker.

The sovereignty of God strikes me just now. It strikes me when I think of the broad strokes of His story that were played out by this servant of His. All rulers are like pawns on a chess board. Willingly or unwillingly they play out God's plan for His creation. A king's heart is God's tool. He steers it like a rudder. Didn't the Persian King Cyrus say that Jerusalem would never be rebuilt? Wasn't he the same king who later not only changed his mind, but supplied Nehemiah's project to rebuild the walls of Jerusalem? What about the signers of the Declaration of Independence? Weren't they all skeptics at first?

At Nixon's funeral, the Reverend Billy Graham said that Winston Churchill's funeral was an event arranged by Churchill himself. In the ceremony, a bugle played taps to signal the end of an era. After that, another bugler played reveille to signal the beginning of a new era. We've played taps. The soldiers of our country and our faith are now either at rest or onto other assignments. Their time in our presence, immediate or global, is now over. Let us now look to our new leaders, and let us not forget that they are in the hands of the supreme Leader of all time, the God of creation, Guide of history. Play reveille!!

Tell me what you think, I'm just thinkin out loud.

Define Yourself

I found it interesting recently that a pastoral search committee of a local church found it necessary to have the members of the church define the church. What did they want that for? It seemed an odd request then, but not now. What the committee members wanted was to know who they were representing as a church. What was its personality? Was it conservative, liberal, evangelical, orthodox? *Who* was the church?

Herein is an assessment of a body of people that has an application to people as individuals. I have come to know myself as a creative individual by the pleasure I have taken in creating. I, direct and produce video, and act and speak, and I love doing those things. What did my intense enjoyment in these activities tell me? They helped me realize that I was created as a creative individual. I love all the expressions that I have a talent for. I am driven in my heart not only to create, but to serve the living God with these abilities.

There is an old piece of advice that says "Know thyself". Its good advice. I think a major phase of it is "Define thyself". Identify your strengths, weaknesses, drives, gifts, loves, hates, talents, tendencies etc. Ask yourself "What manner of person did God make me to be?" Is math agreeable with me? Does literature appeal to me? Sometimes you will find a talent for something that you did not know was there. Once you begin to get answers, follow the exhortation of Romans 12: 1,2 and see what God can do with you and your talents.

It will take discipline and devotion to carry this through to full self-realization, but those are the flesh hooks that keep living sacrifices on the altar.

So go, therefore, and know thyself. But it would not hurt to first *define* thyself. This may take a while, so give it some time, and some thought.

Tell me what you think; I'm just thinking out loud.

Another Fine Mess?

The seeming disasters of our lives, the intrusions, impositions and the like can sometimes get us to muttering one of the more famous lines in comic cinema" Well, here's another fine mess you've gotten me into".

Say you wanted to go to a favorite restaurant, but the parking lot was full, and you had to settle for a cafeteria elsewhere. And when you got there, got food and sat down, you sat down with friends you found there. Lo and behold, one of them picks up your ticket and won't let you pay. Yet, while you looked for that parking place a while ago, you muttered. You didn't get what you wanted. Who's in charge?

Write a piece for a publication, turn it in and the editor comes out looking like a human paper shredder. Who's in charge?

Maybe we should harken to Jeremiah 18, vv. 5&6.

While it is commendable and recommended that a believer be an avid student of the ways and Word of God, let not the believer think he has a handle on the whole counsel of God, especially to think that the ways of God can always be predicted. Such an attitude can lead to pride and, ultimately, disappointment and confusion.

It is foolishness to think that a totally committed

believer won't be imposed upon, spat upon, and deprived of home, health, and family. If you think differently, go read the book of Job.

Don't stay mad at the person who crosses you. They're not in charge.

Don't stay mad at God; you're not either.

Tell me what you think, I'm just thinkin out loud.

Do You Love Yourself?

"If you really knew me, you wouldn't like me." This was the comment of a caller to a talk show, and it is all too common among people. What sort of life breeds this state of mind? Basically, it would seem very believable for this to come from a person who does not know Christ as Savior, but it is very prevalent among believers, as well.

The big difference is an active effort by the Holy Spirit to wean that person away from this conviction. First of all, God loves us as a Creator loves His Creation, but believers are the apple of His eye, and have a special attention from Him. Psalm 32:8 tells us what that He will guide us with His eye upon us, but even then we sin. When we sin, we hate ourselves for it. The particular way out of this circle is the ceasing from the sin. God will use all manner of means to accomplish it, and accomplish He will. Believers have a peculiar spiritual ability, the ability *not* to do what we want, when it is bad.

One reason believers come closer to God over time is that they see more clearly just how ugly the heart is. Then they see also more clearly that they are loved by the One who knows that heart better than they do.

It's a long way from hating self to hating a sin nature, but loving oneself. God's love, grace and discipline carry us from one point to the other. The rate of growth is only partially up to us. We choose the natural or supernatural and, most of the time, live with the choices, but, even then, grace can overrule. Choosing to do naturally will eventually land us in the woodshed, because of Phil. 1:6. Choosing the supernatural act is a climb and a battle with the Devil and our own nature, to be sure. We're no match for either, but guess who is? Nevertheless, this choice leads to a peaceful fruit of righteousness for which we can love ourselves. So tell me, do you love yourself?

Tell me what you think, I'm just thinking out loud.

<u>Who</u> are <u>You</u>?

"Jesus we know, and Paul we have heard of, but who are you?"

Among early Memphis broadcasters there are legends known as Hoyt Wooten stories. Here's my favorite:

One day Bob went to Channel 3 studios looking for a job. Channel 3 was in the basement of a hotel in those days, and took some looking for to find. After finding the studio, Bob had to find someone to help him find the personnel manager. This wasn't easy. He ended up walking into the studio area where there was a rather ordinary-looking man in a plaid shirt sweeping the studio floor. He asked the man where the personnel manager might be, and the man led him to the right office. After some discussion, the manager decided he needed Bob's services, but had to get the consent of the **BOSS**. He led Bob back out to the studio area and introduced him to the ordinary-looking man in the plaid shirt, sweeping the studio floor who just happened to be Hoyt Wooten, the owner of the station.

You can be a thorough professional, very good at what you do, but don't let your head become the Goodyear Blimp. Be janitor, or whatever other seemingly common job title there is to be, and do whatever is needed to keep things going well around you. It might put a hatpin in your ego, and it might give you some perspective into what other people and activities support your task.

So be a janitor once in a while. After all, we're all just servants on borrowed time, in a borrowed world.

Tell me what you think, I'm just thinkin' out loud.

The One and Only Original

It is incredible to consider that in any snowfall, every flake is different. While there are obvious and hidden similarities, there is also the uniqueness, the part that sets apart.

The uniqueness of God as a one and only being is mirrored in many different parts of His creation. Snow is one, as we have just discussed, and humanity is another. We're similar and we're different; Two pair of matching bookends, different as night and day. Our talents, gifts, and abilities make us the perfect choice for one task, not so good for another. But the one thing we are most excellent at is being ourselves. We make a first rate us and a second rate anybody else.

In the early part of the century, a filmmaker left his hometown to be a director in a major Hollywood studio. None of the studios was interested, however. Out of patience and money, the man went and made the kind of films he knew how to make. He and his brother started a studio and created a successful series, which impressed the distributor so much he ordered eleven more episodes. This man ended up losing that series to the distributor, but that didn't stop Walt Disney, because by then he knew his niche.

On the way home from the court fight over the first series, he dreamed up another series about a mouse and the rest is history. All this confusion and sorrow he had known earlier eventually led to a success he could never dream at the time. And all this happened because he went to his known strong point.

A young music student named George, who wanted to understudy a great composer of his time, be his apprentice, approached him. The elder musician consented, but advised against it. "You'd be a second rate -------- when you could be a first rate Gershwin", he said.

Confidence has its place, obviously, but the attitude needs holding that no one has anything but what the Creator, God, has given. The unique blend of attributes that make up you make for a no less unique expression of talent in whatever area it exists. Finding that area takes a studied assessment of abilities, discussion with a close friend who knows you well, and a teachable spirit.

So, when you read a biography about someone notable that you like and favor in some area, read to your heart's content. Follow the good examples you see, and you'll learn a lot, but don't be a clone, a carbon copy. Be the one and only original you.

A TIME OF REMEMBRANCE

A popular Christian song of the mid 70's was a tune called "In Remembrance of Me". It was designed to be sung whenever the Lord's Supper is served. "In Remembrance of Me" is a phrase taken right out of Scripture spoken by Christ to His disciples in the Upper Room. Why did they need to be told to remember Him? Weren't all those miracles and parables enough to earn Him a place in history if not in their hearts?

A Jewish year is literally dotted with feasts, festivals and holidays. What is the need?

A superstructure of a bridge is a collection of beams and girders all supporting each other and, collectively, reinforcing by upholding, a pathway over impassable terrain or water, or both. Why is all that steel necessary?

God knows the human heart. What did he tell Moses before He took him home? He told him that Israel would abandon her God.

Feasts, festivals and holidays were designed to keep in front of the wayward heart of Israel a constant re-enforcement. This re-enforcement was accomplished by upholding her faith through remembrance of a faithful God in her present who had delivered her in her past. Feasts and festivals were instituted by God to point to His faithfulness.

Girders and beams of steel overhead make a roadway safe for load bearing below by constantly upholding the weight of the span. This re-enforces its ability to carry the load all along the length of the span.

The burden of upholding the weight of traffic on the bridge is supported via closely spaced connections to the steel above. In the same way, the faith of Israel was supported throughout the year via frequent reminders of God's faithfulness to her.

The best support that faith has is evidence that it works. The re-enforcement of her faith by remembrance was Israel's best reason to keep on trusting Him in spite of armies of enemies. God's path for Israel led her straight into the face of those armies, so feasts and festivals were necessary to maintain her faith in Him. Likewise, a collection of steel beams overhead makes a bridge roadway capable of carrying its load.

But Remembrance does more than support and re-enforce faith. It rebukes pride. It reminds someone that God was there for them, and that they could not have made it on their own. This has to happen fairly often to keep one's feet on the ground, off of a false floor called self-confidence. A remembrance of Passover kept Israel aware that God's provision was the only one that worked. Either Israel remembered her God or He reminded her. David numbered the tribes of Israel, placing his confidence in numbers. God took away the numbers to remind him of his misplaced confidence. An army of men fights a battle with warships, airplanes and combat soldiers. Here is a picture of total reliance on human ability, skills, and outright physical strength. An army of God fights a spiritual battle with prayers and praises. Here is a picture of total confidence in God. Whatever God provides is all that a believer has-- or needs. REMEMBER THAT!

Tell me what you think, I'm just thinkin out loud.

It's good for what's *bugging* you!

When the weight of the world is coming down on you, Satan wants it so much to be something you can't put your finger on, and right away you may not. But try to think of why you are feeling so bad, what does not look so good, what looks hopeless, what went wrong and why. When things were right, why? The answer may lie in something you cannot have anymore, so let God take you in His direction for your life.

Circumstances are always in the hands of a completely sovereign God, and the only way to have peace is to believe that. Since He runs things, and things don't agree with you, take that disagreement up with Him. He may or may not change circumstances, but He WILL give you His peace, so you can stand it in your heart. He *will* take the storm out of you before He takes you out of the storm!

An important technique for handling worry and depression is to try to list everything that bothers you. Write all of the concerns down. Disappointments, fears, doubt, you name it, they all need listing. Then pray over each one. The first of two Philippian Bible verses (4:6,7) addresses the natural bent to worry. It suggests taking the energy invested in worrying and encourages the worrier to redirect it to prayer. The second verse (v.7) addresses the anxiety attending each concern. Some bothers cause a lot of worry and pain, some a little. Whatever the pain, God promises that He will trade the problem and its pain for His peace. He gets the stress, you get the peace. The peace will maybe come very soon, maybe later, but it always comes, but only as the problem is truly released from your mind. Remaining stress over days only serves as a reminder that it is not lifted up. I Peter 5:7 also helps.

Now the stress will only leave over time; it may still maybe there immediately after the prayer, but only for a short time afterwards. It usually did not get there in a hurry, it won't leave in one either.

Also some pain is so deep and so strong; you may need to find a friendly ear to share it with. Then the two of you can pray about it, maybe with a little discussion first. They might come up with an angle, a line of reasoning that helps you handle it better. Remember an old corollary, though: the conversation never strays to prayer. Do it! It's good for what's bugging you.

Tell me what you think, I'm just thinkin out loud!

The Carrot

The proclamation of the Gospel is a mandatory exercise for believers. The Gospel is a statement of fact involving a provable historical event, the resurrection of Jesus Christ from death itself! It is not to be sold to them, made desirable thru some human reasoning, as that would cheapen it by bringing it down to man's level.

I think there is a lot of truth in that. What God says is not subject to man's own opinion of it. It does stand on its own as Divine Truth.

Yet there is a carrot, it seems. I continually heard in Young Life meetings that God had a plan. That sounded then, and still does sound like salesmanship to me. Look at Jeremiah 29:11: "I know of the plans that I have for you, " sayeth the Lord, "Plans for welfare and not for calamity to give you a future and a hope". You mean the fact of John 3:16 is not enough? In a sense, it is. Yet there is the carrot, the offering of the idea that God has a way of living that skirts disaster, it says. And it is offered to you along with the rest of the Gospel.

Oh and there's more. Look two verses later, at verse 13: " You will seek Me and find Me when you seek Me with all of your heart" Now the carrot is lifted and you have to reach with all that is in you to get it. Not only that, you have to keep lifting. It takes <u>everything</u> in you, <u>all</u> of your desire, <u>all</u> of your energy, <u>all</u> of your devotion, <u>all</u> of the time! No half hearted desire, no eye on the pleasures of the world, will allow you to have this carrot. The sinful nature of man prevents him from reaching this outright, which is why God has to reach out and offer grace to see this through, but when we draw near to God he draws near to us. No, you won't become a block of salt if you don't, but you might as well be. Without the plans of God active and effective in your life, what kind of life will you have?

So, you have it, the carrot and the condition. If you want the one, you have to satisfy the other. But this verse speaks to believers, those who have already received salvation by faith in God's accomplished work at Calvary.

Tell me what you think, I'm just thinking out loud.

Right There Where You Are

Nothing addresses the uniquely personal need of an individual believer in Jesus Christ and at the same time demonstrates the corporate need of a body of believers like a sermon. A person with a message for a body of believers addresses that group with a message that God has laid on his heart to speak about- and everybody in earshot needs to hear it. It's an amazing demonstration of Divine sovereignty. Get the people there and speak to them. God does it all!

But in the midst of this corporate gathering there is this unique touching of the Holy Spirit in each individual heart. Only God would know who needed to hear the message. Sometimes the people wander into a church and sit down in a pew without knowing why they are there-until they hear the sermon. Some come and sit down with the attitude of the sixties-"Sock it to me, God". All were there.

In the miracles of Christ, the method of reaching people was always the same: Meet the need *they* felt was paramount, then bring them to their most important need as Christ saw it. Meet them at their agenda, and bring them over to His. But He always met them right there where they were first. The individual need of a human heart is always paramount to the Maker of that heart. You could be part of a worldwide audience watching Billy Graham weeks or years after a sermon was preached, but God touched your heart right then and there, and your need was addressed and met. It's the personal touch of a personal God-right there where you are!

Tell me what you think, I'm just thinkin out loud.

God's Golden Warriors

Gold gets a lot of attention in the Bible. God's really into it. He covered *everything* with it. Read the latter chapters of Leviticus concerning the Temple construction, and you'll see what I mean. God wanted everything gold-plated. Gold this, gold that-even Heaven will have streets of Gold.

Solomon's Temple, an expression of praise for God in the heart of his father David, had 600 talents (4500 lbs.) in the most interior room alone. This Holy of Holies was a goldie of goldies at over a million dollars per square foot in today's prices. (Gold priced @ $1700/ounce) No WONDER the excavation efforts were so well attended- everybody wanted some of that. Not even Egypt's King Tut was this well fixed!

God will even have golden warriors-us. Through the trials, the breaking, and the pain, *we* endure and grow in the direction of growing selflessness and flexibility in His Hands.

Gold has a measure of softness. 1 carat is the hardest, 24 carats the softest. God takes us in both directions. We become hard in the testing and tempting, and soft in the breaking and molding. Depending on

His specific purpose for us He makes us to whatever level we need to be to function the best.

So, in all of our trials and travails we are reminded of Job, all of whose problems led him to say, "When He has tried me, I shall come forth as gold".

Tell me what you think, I'm just thinkin out loud.

Smart Stuff!

The technology of this age is far beyond mind-boggling; it's becoming downright unnerving. This is not to say that the design of things that "know" what they are is bad, but where does it go from here?

In the March 1998 issue of Cadalyst Magazine, there is a section about AutoDesk, the company that invented AutoCad, the Cadillac of design software. The technology of design, an article in this section points out, is moving toward "model based design". When designing a car, you will no longer draw lines, arcs and circles, but instead, you design the wheels, bumpers and other parts as whole parts. Furthermore, these objects incorporate "design intent". A door, for example, would have certain characteristics that make it a door and not just a set of lines. These characteristics would include dimensions and motions, as well as how the object would interact with other objects adjacent to it.

These are objects with souls, almost. Intellect is the ingredient here. The thing created knows what it is, what it is supposed to do, how to do it, etc. This is a ways further than smart missiles, those computer guided warheads that can pick which bathroom to take out.

All of this technology is for industry and commerce, you understand. But let the next wicked world ruler get a hold of it, and the created monster has had some serious plastic surgery; He may no longer look nearly as bad or dangerous as he used to - but he is, and then some.

The level and advent of technology at any time are sometimes scary to see, but we who look to what the future holds need also to look to Him who holds the future!

Tell me what you think, I 'm just thinkin out loud.

Life's Best Tribute

"Goodbye England's Rose, may you ever grow in our hearts,
you were the grace that placed itself where lives were torn apart,
You called out to our country, and you whispered to those in pain... "

Such was the tribute paid to none less than a goddess in her day, Lady Diana Spencer. She deserved the comments given her by Bernie Taupin, Elton John's lyricist.

Her mixture of sins and good deeds can stand as reminder and encouragement that, while we have our most grievous sins, we also have the chance to make a beautiful difference in the lives of others.

It was interesting that another who whispered to those in pain, Mother Teresa, also went to her reward just a few days after Diana did. God seemed to want to make a statement about altruism by the dual publicity given these two on their passing.

I am reminded of a radio spot in which Garrison Keillor, the host of Public Radio's "Prairie Home

Companion", notes that people won't be remembered by what they accumulated. Stuff means nothing. It's what's done with stuff that counts. Lady Di had a lot, and she did a lot of good with it. Mother Teresa did what she could with what she had, which was never much. Resources are never really the issue, it's what you do with them that matters.

It makes you wonder, how do you want to be remembered? The radio spot ends with a very good line: "To all of you who have already donated time and money, thanks so much for all you've done, imagine what more could do." Just imagine.

Tell me what you think, I'm just thinkin out loud!

An Occasional Reminder

A wrecker wasn't needed to place a wheel truck under a boat trailer axle so the trailer could be towed. The axle had worked out of the hub during transit, but the end of the axle stayed in the recess of the wheel and rode there with the wheel spinning against it at 40 mph! With turns and stops and starts for who knows how long, the trailer, with a 1500-pound boat on top, arrived at the destination, and the axle just stayed in the recess part of the hub. The trailer arrived where it was towed, making noises, but those noises were never investigated until the trip was over. What, or rather Who, kept it there?

Firemen were not called to a kitchen fire caused by a piece of cheese falling onto a toaster element, which sparked a tiny flame. The flame died tiny, instead of also igniting whatever else was in the toaster. Why?

"The mind of man plans his way, but the Lord directs his steps". But the steps of human feet are not the only thing directed. How about looks? How about the "chance" glance inside the toaster when the cheese dropped and ignited? It was a candle flame blown out with a breath, but only with Divinely sovereign timing was it that way.

Such events are part and parcel of Divine sovereignty. It's a Holy protection. It's *Awesome*!

Tell me what you think, I'm just thinkin out loud!

The Spreadsheet Gospel

Day 1	$0.01	
	$0.02	
	$0.04	**Life has its choices**
	$0.08	
	$0.16	
	$0.32	
1 week	$0.64	
	$1.28	
	$2.56	**what's yours?**
	$5.12	
	$10.24	
	$20.48	
	$40.96	**Would you like**
2 weeks	$81.92	
	$163.84	**$100,000.00**
	$327.68	
	$655.36	**RIGHT NOW?**
	$1,310.72	
	$2,621.44	**or**
	$5,242.88	
3 weeks	$10,485.76	**a penny**
	$20,971.52	
	$41,943.04	**a day**
	$83,886.08	
	$167,772.16	**re-doubled**
	$335,544.32	
	$671,088.64	**every day**
	$1,342,177.28	
	$2,684,354.56	**for 30 days?**

Day 30

$5,368,709.12 **Think about it**

This ain't about

$$$ MONEY $$$

Its about your **soul!**

Where's it gonna be in 30 days, Guaranteed?

BY WHOM? **JOHN 3:16 IS A GUARANTEE!** **THINK ABOUT IT!**

Idea adapted from Walker Texas Ranger, Thanks, Chuck
Tell me what you think, I'm just thinkin out loud.

Getting Better All the Time

In this world where the seeker of unpopular truth is heavily derided, the Prophet John of the Bible has a lot of common stock with the investigator Ken Starr. Ken maybe had dirt on just a few people. The Gospel writer John has the goods on us all. The evidence to support Ken Starr's conclusions will be spun into the ground as soon as the world press can get to it. Ken Starr's findings concern what may have happened, while John's concern is what is and what is to be. Look at what John said would happen in these last days.

Spin this: Debit cards are replacing checks, banking conglomerates are getting more conglomerate! Large companies are getting larger, and fewer. The present day economy is ushering in an age unequalled in unevenness of wealth. The rich are getting super rich, the poor are getting poorer, and the middle class is getting squeezed. As this Divine creation wanders farther and farther away from its Creator, it gets more and more lost, and listens to more and more confusing voices. The system we know as the world is coming unraveled, like the loose end of a rope. The separated strands are getting longer and longer.

As time goes by, it has to be said that God is a God of ever more amazing grace, given the growing numbers and types of sin He puts up with. A pro football player/preacher spoke God's Truth on an issue and almost lost his commercial endorsements because the companies did not want to offend anybody.

To the world, the general direction of this society is all about money. To me it's all about grace, and it just keeps getting better all the time!

Tell me what you think, I'm just thinkin out loud!

Don't Ski Into a Tree!

The year 1998 was marked by two totally avoidable tragedies involving famous people: They both skied right into a tree!

They both were involved in a harmless fun activity, when some side pleasure distracted them. They paid no attention to their direction, had no ability to stop or turn away in time, and WHAM! It's over.

What is the direction in your life? Is it helpful, fun, and getting you where you want to go? Watch it! Don't ski into a tree! Don't let some side distraction take you somewhere you shouldn't go, and grab you so you can't turn away or stop before its too late. Don't ski into a tree!

There is a way that seems right unto a man, but in the end it is the way of death! Is the goal in your life clear? Do you know where you are headed? Is it good for you? Then watch it, and stay on the path to it, and wait for it to run its course and yield its fruit. Do not turn aside for quicker pleasure. Get to the bottom of the mountain, claim Jeremiah 29:11 for <u>your</u> life. The best things are worth waiting for, but sometimes it takes waiting and diligent watching to get there.

Watch yourself, watch your life; don't ski into a tree!

Tell me what you think; I'm, just thinkin out loud!

Don't Miss It!

Usually a pleasurable event will be advertised by its promoter with the catch line "Don't Miss It!"

But so much of life's joy is missed when we act so strongly to avoid its pain.

Happiness is all too often misidentified as being a guaranteed part of the Christian experience. This is because of the human desire to avoid pain at all cost. It's a natural reflex, but it sometimes has to be relaxed to allow a deeper experience of hurt, and its outcome. Sometimes we cannot avoid the pain, sometimes we can. But always it has an effect. Our willingness to accept it determines the reaction.

My dear Scottish friend, Kristine Gibbs, has endured two severe cerebral hemorrhages, and written a book about the recovery from the second one. She writes" Slowly, in (the) hospital, I began to comprehend that our capacity for joy and pain are one. You cannot appreciate one without experiencing the other".

Our tragedy is not that we suffer, but that we waste suffering. We waste the opportunity it provides for depth, growth, compassion and understanding.

Following Christ does not mean exclusion from the world's pain, but that one will be given strength to bear whatever comes. Paul wrote in 2 Cor. 4:8 ' we are afflicted in every way, but not crushed; perplexed but not driven to despair; persecuted, but not forsaken; struck down, but not destroyed' ".

When a caterpillar goes into a cocoon, it is protected, strengthened and generally made ready for the rest of its life. His crawling days are over, and he is being made ready to fly and be appreciated as a beautiful part of God's Creation.

There is a scene in the Billy Graham movie, "Joni", that seems applicable. She is sitting in a wheelchair conversing with someone else in a wheelchair. She says that she would sooner be in a wheelchair knowing Him, than walking around, not (knowing Him). It took a long time for her to arrive at that conclusion, but it was a knee jerk response to his negative statement about God that she had just heard.

Its His Joy God is steering us toward- Don't Miss It!

Tell me what you think, I'm just thinkin out loud!

It's not a buffet!

Down in Dillard Ga., at the Dillard Inn, when you dine, you sit down at the dinner table and the server brings out all that's available to eat. You just spoon or fork out what you want on to your own plate and leave the rest.

In calendar keeping the astronomers take a well-known rule of thumb that every fourth year is a leap year, and go further. Not only are the years divisible by four the leap years, but also they are not leap if they are divisible by 100 UNLESS also divisible by 400! What an excruciating piece of timekeeping! What's the point? Why the diligent adherence?

We take what we want off the plate of creation and Divine provision and leave the rest. We all live like we are eating in Georgia, at that inn. We assign calendars a certain way, because we see an acute need to keep in perfect lockstep with the movement of earth and sun. We don't mind adherence to movement, but don't make us walk so narrowly, or live so submissively. "We will let you design our days, Lord, but don't go messin with our diets" We have our diets for greed, lust, and forget about anything that keeps us from having it all. Isn't that what advertising entices us to do- have it all?

We have just got to have the fancy cars, the ski resorts, the delicacy food, and the things we have just GOT to have. We have all just got to have elbowroom. Doing, having and being become a cancer, never stopping in their paths. Give us love and Your Spirit, and leave off the hell and damnation, fire and brimstone.

The problem with this is that it's not a buffet we are given in life. God made us creatures of choice, but He also assigned consequences to the choices. He made the world and laid out the rules for it. Yes, He allows bad things to happen to bad and good people. Yes, He allowed a serpent to convince a woman who convinced a man, and, yes, they got thrown out of the garden for their choices. They had choices and they had direction. They did their thing, He did His.

We love astronomy, we just choke on accountability.

Tell me what you think, I'm just thinkin out loud!

We've been to the moon and back! *Now* where are we?

When I graduated high school, it was like leaving a known, stepping into an unknown. No more cocoon, no more acid rock. The Fifth Dimension said it was the dawning of the Age of Aquarius. Mystic crystal revelation, and the mind's true liberation were the stated ingredients of the near future. Question: Liberation from what?

There was a problem they didn't address in all that fancy singing. How was it going to be in our hearts? How were we going to respond to the future? Evidently they'd hoped we'd buy all this stuff and wait. We would wake up and see new ways of dealing with old problems. We did and we didn't. Science got a lot better. Electronics got a lot smaller. Computers shrank from a large room to a laptop. But crime stays on, embarrassing us all the more. We got so embarrassed, we quit calling it crime. Gimme the sex, forget about the kid.

The singers forgot about the heart. They forgot about prejudice, about poverty, greed and every human lust. They left them out of the lyrics, but we still have em. The new age of enlightenment just became the pawn of the intelligent people with bad hearts who used it against others. Now all around you, it's just about the money. Sports, politics, you name it, its all gone to greed, to seed.

Aquarius, where are you?

Tell me what you think, I'm just thinkin out loud.

The Forgotten Element

Sales people have an inspirational booklet they can receive called "Bits and Pieces". It's full of quotes and sayings that help invigorate the mind and heart, give people reason to have hope, try harder, etc. It's written to inspire, and it generally does a very good job. It seems that certain words of other people have a way of impacting lives. That's interesting, very interesting.

The ability of one person to affect another for good or bad is reflected in Scripture, with the commands to be light and salt in the world, that other people might see your good works and praise your God. Do they praise your god when they don't hear them? Yes, they do. Your god lets them off the hook, relieves them of their accountability to the one true God. Who's your god?

Dr. Maxie Dunnam, a former president of Asbury Theological Seminary in Kentucky, said the doctrine of personal holiness was the most neglected doctrine in Protestant Christianity. This has been a very convicting statement for me lately. Actions come from the thoughts and drives of the heart as much as words, and speak with louder volume than words. Where have I been lately, and what have I been seen doing? Which god or God do those actions praise, or cause others to?

A nationally known Gospel group has an interesting feature. A fellow worker said recently that their stagehands had the best dirty jokes he had ever heard. I feel badly for the singers to have it said that their own associates had not taken in the truth of their own called work. Where is the message coming unraveled, what's not getting through? Are the offhanded comments not staying "salty"?

In the movie "Ten Commandments", the pharaoh returns to the palace and says to his wife "Israel's god is God". He has just witnessed the total annihilation of his army in the Red Sea, and the deliverance of Israel from his clutches. Who is your god? What effect is it having on those around you?

Tell me what you think, I'm Just Thinkin out Loud.

Patterns, Examples and Legacies

Easy Eddie was Al Capone's accountant. He kept Big Al looking squeaky-clean to the law in the midst of the racketeering, murder, and a mob machine that ran Chicago's South Side in the 1920's and 30's. After all that had happened, all that the mob had done, the only charge the Feds could nail Al with was tax evasion. As it turned out, Easy Eddie helped.

Easy Eddie met a lady, fell in love, got married, and they had a boy, they nicknamed Butch. Butch was a harmless infant, but he had a big impact on Eddie. Fatherhood made him sit up and look at what he was doing, and what it would be like to raise a kid. He decided he was going to do the right thing by Butch, so he turned state's evidence and testified against Al Capone in court. Usually turning state's evidence might get you fired, but this was the mob he turned against. Pretty soon, Easy Eddie got fitted for some cement shoes, and there was no more Eddie.

Butch saw all this, knew what his dad died for, and it made a deep impression. He grew up and became a pilot, flying a fighter during World War II. It came his turn to do something heroic. He did it, and the film on his warplane's camera bore it out. Chicago named an airport after war hero Butch- O'Hare Airport.

The life you are leading is an example. The pattern is being set, your legacy is being lived, whether in broad strokes or little moves or words. What conclusions will be drawn about what is important to you? What will it motivate others to do? Will you be Easy Eddie before Butch, or Butch after Easy Eddie? You decide.

Tell me what you think, I'm just thinkin out loud.

What's your Life?

In 1937 MGM Studios released a film starring Janet Gaynor and Adolphe Menjou. It was named "A Star is Born". In 1956 the studio released a film starring Judy Garland and Frederic March.

The name of that film was also "A Star is Born". In 1977 Barbara Streisand was executive producer for a film she starred in opposite Kris Kristofferson. The name of the movie was "A Star is Born".

The plot for all three movies was the same. A nightclub singer was doing her job, making her living, when a star noticed her. The star got real interested in her and started having her perform in bigger venues, with much bigger crowds. The star fell in love with the nightclub singer, and they married. His image of what she could become was what steered the rest of her life, as she realized his vision.

Jeremiah 29:11 strikes me just now in all this. Isn't a believer a lot like the nightclub singer before conversion? Isn't the change which occurs after a person's introduction to Jesus Christ a bit like the change which occurred in the singer's life? The verse I cited reads "For I know the plans that I have for you", sayeth the Lord," plans for welfare and not for calamity, to give you a future and a hope". So, just as the movie had different actors for the same plot, so is the promise of that verse a plan that God has for everyone.

But, if you look at each of the different movies, you will see differences in how the different characters act out their parts. Two become movie stars, one a rock star. Still a plan, a vision, is born and realized, just from a simple introduction. Sound familiar?

The individual details are similar sometimes, but the end result is always one orchestrated by a sovereign God. The individuality and personality of a person are colors on a palette, bringing different strokes not of fate, but Divine Beauty. This is the beauty of the mystery. No one knows quite how, but one introduction makes all the difference in the world.

Tell me what you think, I'm just thinkin out loud.

Gotcha Time!

An old Sony ad really struck a chord with me a long time ago. It was a TV ad for their pocket cassette recorders. In a restaurant, a group of people was seated around a table. They were giving their food orders to a waiter who appeared to be writing them down. As soon as he got all the orders, he went to the kitchen. He then pulled a Sony cassette recorder out of his pocket and laid it on a table. When the food was served, and one or another in the group complained that what they got was not what they ordered, out came the recorder again. Its gotcha time!

If you step out off of a curb, or a raised surface, the law of gravity is going to apply. It will do so regardless of whatever alternative ideas and lifestyles you embrace concerning it. Personal choice has its liberty, but it still has its laws. It does not matter what you think about the law of gravity and its applicability to you. Just step out against it, and you may become a statistic. Its gotcha time!

It seems the world is very much like Old Testament Israel in its most evil days, when every man did what he thought was right in his own mind. But the physical laws that can kill you have spiritual equals that can do the same. Matthew 12:36 says that every word that is spoken in your lifetime will be remembered when your life is over and your body is a cold corpse. God's got a zillion Sonys out there, and He's not missin a word! Its gotcha time!

Be careful, keep your words sweet, make em something you can stand to eat!

Tell me what you think, I'm just thinkin out loud!

Just when you need it most!

One of the most fascinating jobs I have had was driving a forklift for a stage construction crew. In May 2000 I was involved in putting up the stages for Memphis In May, the biggest city festival in the country. My company had been hired to construct the stages for a weekend event called Music Fest, and there were three main stages. Each location had stages of construction that called for different parts. Each started off with square, flat wooden blocks, which the feet stood on. On top of the feet were uprights of varying lengths. The guys on the forklifts were told what to bring and when to bring it, in order to meet the need at that point in the construction.

It took a few days to go from blocks to uprights to a stage, then put up the towers, run cable and hang the roof. But it meant that certain parts came out of a trailer at a certain time and not until then.

We did not unload the roof first thing.

That particular order of materials drew an immediate parallel to Phil. 4:19, and our perception of need. God brings into our lives the materials, experiences, people, and stages we need when we need them. He does not bring in something until it is necessary for us at that moment, and that does not necessarily always jive with our timetable. More than once have I heard of key people in a ministry headed out the door to cancel or shut it down, only to be met at the door with the money needed to make it happen.

Just like the speakers for the house sound on the stage were not delivered early on the site, the plan for our provision is not always what we think it will be or should be. Waiting on God's timing is not an easy thing. But just like the equipment that arrives when it is needed, the needs we have are met just when God says we need them. He is always faithful to His Word, THAT we can count on!

Tell me what you think, I'm just thinkin out loud!

A seed of faith, a shred of hope

It is interesting to look at the miracles of healing in the New Testament and note what made them happen. Jesus did what He did because someone was willing to be healed and was willing to give Jesus a chance to be Himself and do the healing.

How often do we get ourselves into circumstances or get put into them, and start wondering how we are going to get ourselves out? We are like a rat dropped into a maze: we immediately set about wondering how we are going to get out. Sometimes our own resources just are not enough. But something in us feels challenged to figure a way out of the maze all by ourselves.

The woman in the crowd, the lame man, the man dropped in through the roof on a pallet all had one thing in common: They knew that healing was impossible with their own resources or those of other people. This does not make it wrong to seek medical or professional help when it can be an aid. It just makes it necessary for us to accept being at the end of the resources when we get there. Then we cry out, and then we seek the power of the only One who can heal us and help us out.

A seed of faith leading to a shred of hope was all they had back in the New Testament days, but its all they needed. It's all we need.

Tell me what you think, I'm just thinkin out loud!

It's not about elbows!

Did you ever go to a movie theater and notice that there is only one armrest for every two elbows? Of course, an elbow has an armrest all its own at the ends, but in the middle, its timeshare, space share or war while two people are seated adjacent to each other. People watching movies have to compromise over the armrest in order to have peace between them.

But don't carmakers always put in their advertising the phrase, "plenty of elbow room"? It seems part of the American Dream is having all you want, and then some. Elbowroom is just a sign of that great American Dream. But it's not available at the movie theater.

The luxury of "elbow room" is a right, it seems. But at some points, it would appear to be not a right, but a luxury, which indeed it is. In an airliner, you have to pay for a first class or business section seat for elbowroom. When you are watching a movie the only way to guarantee elbowroom is to rent the movie.

People get too wrapped in the little things, when the bigger picture says there are much more pressing needs. That personal expression and comfort are supposed to be low priority items runs counter to the human desire. But didn't God say, "it is better to give than to receive"? Sure doesn't feel as good giving, though, or doesn't it?

It's not about elbows, really. It's about giving up personal space for the sake of people and their eternal destinies. It's about letting some things go, so someone else can just have room to live, and make it to heaven. It's about giving up time and energy to see that they learn how to do just that.

A ship may be safe in its harbor, but the ship was not made to stay there all the time. It was made to venture out, and if it doesn't, it's either retired or in for repair. But it's the venturing out that makes it a stronger ship. The stresses introduced bring out strengths not previously known. So it is with people.

Sometimes you can have elbowroom, sometimes you can't.

Tell me what you think, I'm just thinking out loud!

It's all in a night's work!

First Angel- Elohim, Miracle Dept.

Second Angel- This is Moses' Angel; I got a big order for you today.

First Angel- Well, tell me about it, miracles are the order of business here!

Second Angel- He's got some 2-3 million people with him headed southeast out of Egypt, and we need some major help!

First Angel- Oh yeah, where's he going with this flock?

Second Angel- Up around the Sea of Galilee, eventually. Right now we've gotta get em out of Egypt.

First Angel- Where's he headed now?

Second Angel-Baal Zephon, which puts him in a hard spot. He has the mountains on one side, the sea on the other, and the Egyptian Army behind him if he doesn't get them out of there now! He's got somewhere between 2-3 million people and they need to get out of the country in 12 hours or less. Then we have to come up with a place to rest and provide catering for this crowd.

First Angel- well, don't get excited. We can handle this. Just have Moses raise his staff at the shoreline and we will move water and dry up mud in a hurry to make about a 3-mile wide path. That oughta do it in time! We'll even clear out the sand crabs!

Second Angel- That's a good start. Now how about lodging? These folks are gonna be tired and hungry after all that walking.

First Angel- Well, they are going into a desert area, so 750 square miles is not difficult real estate to round up, at least not for now.

Second Angel- You're gettin there! Now how about the food?

First Angel- Well, Divine Providence will put a few million birds in the area, and park em' near a wooded area so the folks can light fires and cook the birds.

Second Angel- Look what are we gonna do if the Egyptian Army comes into the space after them?

First Angel- Well, that means it can't be wading water, because we have to drown a mounted army. Don't worry, it will be so obviously a miracle that the sea was split three miles wide in the first place. I'll post some angels in back and they'll keep the Egyptians under control. Don't worry about them.

Second Angel- Gee, thanks for taking care of us!

First Angel- Hey buddy, you called on Elohim. It's all in a night's work!

It's the Working!

If world history has an abundance of anything, it is overflowing with demonstrations of Divine Power. There is a long list of situations designed for evil purposes turned into good ones. Romans 8:28 brings this out when it says that all things WORK for the good of all that love Him and are called according to His purposes.

A rapist attacked a young woman, and she later gave birth to a girl. Instead of forever letting that hang over her, that girl, Ethel Waters, became a Gospel singer and was heard at many a Billy Graham Crusade in the 70's. Starting off as a nightclub singer, she was later touched in her heart and gave her voice to the One who had touched her.

Adolph Hitler wanted to evangelize the world with Naziism. He planned and built a huge broadcast center near the Mediterranean Sea. But before he could ever use those powerful transmitters and massive towers, Nazi Germany was conquered. The broadcast center became the central point for reaching Europe with the Gospel under the direction of Trans World Radio.

Bad things happening, bad things being put in motion doesn't always mean bad endings. God allows the evil people to do their bidding and then steps in at His appointed time and gets what He wants out of it. So the bad thing gets turned into a good one in His time. The verse doesn't use the word happen; it uses the word WORK, implying the passage of time.

The outworking of Jesus Christ dying on a cross was that sinful people could get a ticket to Heaven. Just because He lets people start bad, doesn't mean they're going to end up that way. Ethel Waters didn't profess faith as a child and stay that way from then on. But she ended her days on that note.

It's not the start that matters, its how it turns out- It's the Working!

Tell me what you think, I'm just thinkin out loud!

I Stand Amazed!

There are some situations in the physical and spiritual worlds that truly amaze me! Some things happen, and I just never can figure out how they work, but they do.

When a Federal Express jetliner takes off at the Memphis, Tennessee airport, it's lifting close to 200,000 lbs of metal off the ground! This happens when the air over the top of the wing gets stretched out. It has a longer distance to travel over the wing than the air under it, so the air on top gets stretched out, creating a vacuum. The vacuum pulls up on the wing, and the plane flies! But it sure is carrying a lot of metal, plastic and rubber when it does! It's truly amazing!

A long time ago, someone was born in circumstances considered dubious at best, socially. The so-called father heard that his intended was already pregnant, so he tried quietly tried to have her put in a convent. The kid was born, though. The parents apparent raised him, loved him, watched him grow up and have a ministry of healing and teaching. For his premiere ministry event, he had water gathered in huge tubs and he turned it into wine, the best wine the partygoers had had all evening. ("Move over Moinhos, this is DIVINE stuff heah!"). What a party saver! Then there was the dead man who got up and walked out of his grave on this guy's command. This man lived perfectly, committing no sins, and then got <u>hung</u> for it! But the most amazing part is that the real father considered that the sins of past, present and future humanity were paid for in that one crucifixion!

These two amazing things were both brought about by one amazing God. He created the physical circumstances that put planes in the air, and the spiritual circumstances that put His creation back in contact with Himself! It was the next best thing to Eden.

Tell me what you think, I'm just thinkin out loud!

Don't shoo em', shoot em!

Sometimes when people make decisions and take action accordingly, there are consequences they may not like that they may have to face later on as a result. Consequences also come from not having made a decision and taken action. Quite often the consequences are likened to birds. When we do something to delay the consequences, we shoo the birds away. But sooner or later, they come to roost back with us, and we can no longer delay the results of the choices we made earlier. Putting off a decision is, in itself, an active decision to shoo the birds away. But they come back and sometimes it's too late to shoo them off again.

For many years in high school I heard the Gospel, as presented by Rollin Wilson, a tireless crusader for teen souls. Rollin has been sharing the Gospel message through Young Life meetings for over five decades. But I kept putting it off, shooing the birds away. I was given the chance to decide for Christ at many a time, but was not willing. When I finally did make a decision to turn my life over, it was after a three-day relentless pursuit. I had been at the Young Life Ranch in Colorado, and was considering salvation, but just didn't want to. I was tired of the question being put to me in my head, so I finally gave up and did. It was a very hard decision to make, but, once made, it gave me immense peace.

Had I stayed away long enough, I might have died without having made the decision that has changed my life. The birds of consequence were the difficulties I felt from resisting my decision time and time again. But some people die in car wrecks, heart attacks, and any number of other events that take their lives-and their chances to decide- away.

No one knows how many days are appointed him or her. Deal with the consequences of a bad decision by avoiding them altogether. Don't shoo the birds away, shoot em!

Tell me what you think, I'm just thinkin out loud!

Who's your god?

When the Beatle John Lennon made his comment "We're more popular than Jesus", he was not making a comment of self-regard. But his comment was taken that way. He later explained that he had no delusion of that sort. But rather, the adoration he saw showered on the Beatles far outshone any regard he saw shone to any deity.

John Lennon observed a level of devotion in churches he visited, but it never compared to the screaming and clamoring which were constantly thrown at the Beatles. Isn't that an interesting comment that shows believers how they rate in their adoration of their God? Here was an outsider to the faith saying that he felt as if he and his fellow band members enjoyed a devotion from their fans he never saw given to God by his worshippers. It was not just the screaming, either. It was the constant clamoring for more of what they offered.

Take this to our current situation. To a person who is not the least bit interested in the type of relationship we have with our God, what do we do that would make them interested? What turns them off? Who do we show them to be our God, or our god? What do we really worship when we are not in a worship service? The possession of nice, expensive stuff is not a sin, necessarily. The main thing that can mark the difference there is does the stuff own us? If we can lose the stuff and recognize that everything we have is expendable, and that people always matter more, then maybe we can have it after all.

Tell me what you think, I'm just thinkin out loud!

Good ole Peter Pistol Mouth!

The comments of Peter as recorded in the Gospels are usually given as proof that hoof-In-mouth disease has Biblical origins. I have to think that many a theologian has wondered how this "loose cannon" made it into the Gospels, much less the inner sanctum of apostles. A cartoonist rendering might accurately show a snub nose .38-barrel stickin out between the teeth, always with a whiff of smoke coming out, cause its just been shot off!

But there he was, not only in the Gospels, among the apostles, but among those closest to his Lord. This guy never had a guarded comment- he always spoke his heart. Sometimes it got him in trouble; sometimes it got him rebuked, one time it almost got him sunk! Don't we just identify with him about that coat, and that walking on water was one cool stunt. "Here, Lord, let ME try that!"

Peter was such an inspiration to most people because we know that if God would put up with and turn a clown like *that* around, then surely there was hope for us all! Peter had his chance to identify with his Lord when the chips were down- and he turned tail. Human strength has its limits but Godly power knows no limits in a human life that is His.

For pure inspiration and hope, nothing can beat a comparison between the Barney Fife of the apostles and the Bible expositor of his own epistles. It's a clear picture of a work of grace.

Tell me what you think, I'm just thinkin out loud!

Its not gonna work!

A poster I read during college had a message that has stayed with me since I first read it: The society that exalts philosophy as a high art, yet shuns plumbing as a humble practice will have neither good philosophy nor good plumbing. Neither its pipes nor its theories will hold water.

The true merit of a command is its good effect. There are objective physical laws that bring about good results when obeyed, and sometimes tragic results when shirked. When we choose to follow the orders of a physical law we reap the good result of adherence. It means we have submitted to its authority, and have recognized its higher wisdom.

It is this authority and wisdom that are crucial to the obedience to spiritual laws. Disobedience to Scriptural edict says that the disobedient person has the authority to judge the edict, and the wisdom to tell whether or not it is the best decision to obey it. Judging the law extends itself to judging the lawgiver, so the lawbreaker extols him or herself as a god in his or her own right. This is idolatry in its purest form. Idolatry is the same as the sin of witchcraft, it is written.

Get in the face of physical law and you may get away with it from time to time. Get in the face of the God of Spiritual Law, and you always pay for it. Its not gonna work!

Tell me what you think, I'm just thinkin out loud!

It's the Old Faithful!

The world is getting further and further away from its roots of faith in its Creator. It is persecuting in ever-greater numbers those who hold on to their faith in their Creator. It laughs at Christians, makes fun of their stubborn beliefs, calling them outdated.

Outdated, you say? That might be taken to mean that they don't apply anymore, that they are wholly ineffective in dealing with one's affairs and people. Is that so? Is it not, rather, that the trials and tribulations of the world seem time and again to prove the effectiveness of the principles expressed in Scripture? Time and again don't we see evil slay the wicked, fools and their money soon parted, and a host of other verses from Proverbs proven true? It takes some far seeing eyes to see the FINAL outcome of the ways of the world. Romans 8:28 says that things WORK to the good of those who are His.

It takes time to see God's principles for people and their ways to be shown true. One thing a nonbeliever cannot prove is that God does not answer prayer. He cannot prove beyond a reasonable doubt that a Sovereign Being did not intervene to bring about miracles. He cannot prove that God did not bring something to pass that He said He would do.

The world is faithful to the moment. The Scriptures are faithful to the end of time. God's Word is <u>The</u> Old Faithful!

Tell me what you think, I'm just thinkin out loud!

One Empty Trip!

Question: What's the number one question people ask other people after Christmas Day? Answer: What did you get for Christmas? What is the least fulfilling obsession we have about Christmas? What did we get? Well, what did you get?

Christmas comes, Christmas goes, and we have little more to show for it than the stuff under a dressed up tree with our name under the "to" part. That's the world's way of shoving God out of the picture. It's Satan's way of shoving accountability out of the picture. But it is just one empty trip, one unsatisfying experience. Life can be just a series of experiences that we take in, sometimes. It's like throwing pennies down the side of the Grand Canyon. The void inside you just swallows it all up. This goes for doing, having and being.

But there is Someone who can fill up that canyon if we let him. I did the unfulfilling ritual of getting and giving and all and it was one empty trip. It was part of what led me to give somebody else a chance to call my shots. I had the albums I wanted, the girlfriends I wanted, all of it. That was 30 years ago.

If the emphasis of Christmas is on getting, all you get is one empty trip. If it's on the birthday of the One who fills up the inside, then you get something that's worth getting. There the emphasis goes from getting to giving, and that makes it work!

Tell me what you think, I'm just thinkin out loud!

Are You Two?

Deacon Brodie's Tavern sits near the west end of the "Royal Mile" in Edinburgh, Scotland. It is in an interesting location actually, just a block and a half west of where John Knox once held forth at St. Giles Cathedral and two blocks east from Edinburgh Castle. The chief resident of the castle was Mary Queen of Scots, whom Knox often preached against. Brodie's place is right in the middle, which seems appropriate, because he was a bit of both people.

By day, Deacon Brodie was a cabinetmaker and a respected citizen, an upright person. He was even a town counselor, a position not unlike a city councilman today.

But by night, he was described as a drunkard, a robber, a ne'er do well. He was finally caught in the national treasury, but escaped. A letter written by him to a friend in Scotland was traced and he was caught, returned to Scotland, and hung on gallows he had himself built.

So the deacon had two lives going, and a lot of watching out for what he said to whom and when. He had to be careful for exact words to keep the customers from finding out what sort of "business" he was in to after hours. It all caught up to him anyway. The simple act of sending a letter home to Scotland from his hideout was his undoing. It's the simple stuff that catches you up when you lead two lives. There are too many bases to touch, too many words to watch for anybody to keep it up forever.

Lead one life and lead it straight and narrow. Anything else is just too much trouble.

Tell me what you think, I'm just thinkin out loud!

Not Our Way

*Say what you want, nobody fights a fight
Like Gideon's Ragtime Army!*

Army, you say? Yes Army! Gideon was an outright chicken in hiding when he got his draft notice. He was not the least bit interested in a fight, but he was called "Mighty Warrior". Somebody knew something about him that he didn't, apparently.

Gideon was called to lead a mighty army to fight against Israel's enemies. A big difference was this was not a "US and allied forces against Iraq" type of battle, with carpet bombs, smart missiles and all. This was a horn and percussion section, tootin and bangin for all they were worth, only to have the enemy fall out like flies after a spray of insect repellent.

So this "mighty warrior" called an army and had it pared down by God to 300 people to face a much larger army. Yet it happened, they won! How more dramatic proof do we need that the ways of God are not the ways of man? The ways of God call upon His people simply to act in confident belief that He is going to do His part. Not only that, but His part is going to be so crucial to success that it will be clear who caused the victory.

As it was with Gideon, so it is with us!

Tell me what you think, I'm just thinkin out loud!

There's Always a Cloud

When Moses and the nation of Israel finally got all their passports cleared, they got out of Egypt before Pharaoh could realize he had lost his captive labor force. After they cleared the Red Sea, they needed a navigation device to direct their way to the homeland. Their God, I Am, gave them a cloud by day and fire by night to follow. He knew just where they needed to go to get where He wanted them to be.

What was God calling Himself at the burning bush? I Am. Its like He was always there, which He was, and is. The present tense has a way of saying that it never was not, which is what He meant. The Children of Israel were to follow Someone who would always be looking out for them, thus I Am. The cloud was always there during the day to guide them to the land they were to claim. It was always His land, wherever it was, because He made it all, and owned it all. You get a deep sense of stewardship when you understand that.

I Am is still there, still here with us. He walks with us and gives us what we need, leading us in His direction for us, as we ask. Sometimes we get off track and he sets up a new path to work with that. He has maybe a different plan from the original one, but one that serves His purposes. The rockets that take off from Cape Kennedy in the US have computers that do that. We have I Am.

Wherever we walk, the cloud's always there. So's I Am.

Tell me what you think, I'm just thinkin out loud!

Peter's Knee Jerk Gospel

The Apostle Peter rightly gets credit for being the New Testament inspiration of hoof and mouth disease. He was the proverbial knee jerk speaker that often got himself into trouble. But he was also Jesus' right hand guy when it came to a truthful expression. Look at him in John 6, after he has seen a horde of would be followers fall away from his Lord's side. When asked whether the Twelve would also abandon Him, at least then. "Lord, to whom shall we go?', he asks. Ah, but the best is yet to come from this .38 caliber fount of truth " We believe and know that you are the Holy One of God".

A more dilated expression might say " Master we have been by your side this many times and seen the miracles in our own lives as well as the lives of others. We know of no other person or philosophy that can do for people what we have seen You do!" Thus the question in verse 68: "Lord to whom shall we go?"

There is a verse in Proverbs, which says, "out of the mouth comes that which fills the heart". People who are prone to explode in praise at a worship service also show this truth. Peter's life had been changed because of direct contact with life changing Truth, so he was in no position to deny the source of it. He was only ready to speak from a heart of gratitude for what had been done in and for him.

Whether you tapped his knee or pushed his button, Peter knew the truth, and was ready to speak it. Are we?

Tell me what you think, I'm just thinkin out loud!

The Unmistakable Argument

The National Aeronautics and Space Administration, NASA, has been fighting a 30-year fight with skeptics, who say it did not send people to the moon and back. They are still fighting this fight, and one of the interesting aspects of it is the 800 lb. lunar rock collection the astronauts brought home (boys will be boys). The interesting thing about the rocks is that no geologist is disputing their being from the moon.

Given the climate we have here on earth and what it does and has done to rocks here, the lunar rocks show none of those traits.

This, to them, is unmistakable proof that the rocks that were brought here on the space ships came from the moon. They could not look like they did if they had been on earth, the geologists say.

Whenever Israel went to war, God had two things in mind for them: win the battle and make it clear who won it. Looking at the conversations Gideon had with God going into battle, it is apparent that God wanted Israel to have no delusions about the conquest and in whose might it was to be won. For this reason, rather than the usual maces and spears and other military equipment, Israel went to battle with musical instruments. It's sort of like General George Patton fighting WWII with the Boston Pops Orchestra on the front line- yeah right.

But that is precisely the point. The battle line is in the prayer chapel, not the student commons or wherever else the sharing of faith is done. For Gideon and Israel it was the fervent petition and then even more fervent horn blowing that was their part in battle. It is an act of believing faith and obedient action that provides the connection that makes it possible for the heart to be won, or whatever accomplishment is to be done. The believer thus goes forward, knowing clearly who's doing the real fighting.

Unmistakably faithful action makes for unmistakably clear victory and for the clear argument as to who did the winning.

Tell me what you think, I'm just thinkin out loud!

Sometimes you feel like Israel

The nation of Israel was in the grandstand seat to see some of God's greatest triumphs in her behalf. After all didn't He blight Egypt with plagues to convince the king to let them go? Didn't God open the sea up three miles wide to get all 3 million of them through overnight?

God was there for His people, time and time again.

But what wandered through the heart and mind of Israel was a question: "I wonder what big stunt God is going to pull to get us through this one". Israel constantly faced one need or another of one kind or another, and had to be reminded that her God was her protector and provider.

It's the same kind of protection and provision we need today as believers. We are commonly in a Baal Zephon experience- mountains on one side, the sea on the other and the Devil behind us. We wonder what God is going to do to deliver us.

Its not that we have a wavering faith, but just that the edges get dull, the memory fades and we wonder how God will work things out. The challenge ahead is higher than we have ever seen before. We feel like the guy in the New Testament who answered, "Lord I believe, help my unbelief." Sitting in the back of our mind is the question as to whether God will bail us out this time. There is never a question of having enough faith, because that takes the onus off God and puts it on us, as if it was something we could handle alone, or in concert with Him. God gives all the faith we need to face what we face. It's only the matter of being willing to trust and move ahead. With the Army of Egypt behind them there really was not much choice for Israel. There's not much for us either.

It's easy to feel like Israel, wanting to complain about the challenges we face in our lives. But that's not really an option.

Tell me what you think, I'm just thinkin out loud!

Insider out, Outsider in!

Ruth and Esther stand out as the only two women mentioned in Scripture who have books named after them. They came from different backgrounds, but both ended up in the same kind of acclaim. They both preferred an identification that could have been discarded, but one that made a difference for others as well as themselves.

Esther was one whose compassion for her own people led to their survival in the midst of an alien people. Esther's king wanted his wife to perform a dance that she deemed beneath her dignity. She refused and lost her position as queen. A search was started for a replacement. Esther was eventually chosen, and made the new queen. Now Esther had an uncle who made it clear that she was who she was, and where she was in order to save her race from extinction. She was a Jewish maiden married to a gentile king who had been beseeched to destroy her people. Reading the book of Esther really shows a Divine Hand upending the best laid plans of mice and men, as they say. Esther was the insider who went out and saved her people by being among aliens and doing what she only could have done being out.

Ruth was a young gentile widow, by contrast, whose loyalty is oft quoted in wedding vows and other indications of loyalty and love. "Wherever you lodge, I will lodge, wherever you stay, I will stay. Your people will be my people, and your God will be my God." Here was a gentile, an outsider, wanting in, simply because she preferred to be a comfort to her husband's mother. She had seen this woman lose her family. It was this compassion for another that put her among people of another culture. Because of this remarkable love she was sought out and found by her second husband, and became a part of the lineage of Christ Himself. She was the outsider who came in.

The king's heart is as a rudder for God to steer, Scripture says. The hearts of two women were also made a means of saving and steering the Children of God toward His appointed purposes. One woman's heart became part of the path to a Messiah to reconcile God to His chosen people. The heart of the other kept His people alive by avoiding a king's edict of death for them.

History is His Story. The flips and flops of the hand of man are always subject to the steady and sovereign Hand of God.

Tell me what you think, I'm just thinking out loud!

The Great American Myth

When the scientist who discovered the smallpox vaccine first administered it to a patient, he gave the patient cowpox. Your handy Funk & Wagnall's Dictionary describes cowpox as a skin disease found in cattle that when administered to humans, effectively vaccinates them against smallpox. Cowpox is a disease, yes, but a rather harmless disease, and it keeps a patient alive by preventing a killer disease. The bad thing is preventing the worse, in this case.

Most people go through life keeping their noses clean, going to church, doing all kinds of good deeds, and avoiding all kinds of bad ones, thinking this is going to earn them a place in Heaven. They have a moral equivalent of cowpox, called moralism. Moralism has a lot of adherents in the world. It even has an anthem "My Way".

The human psyche, particularly the American (US) one, has this bootstrap mentality that got it out of the Depression and got on with life after WWII. It served a lot of good, getting buildings built, families started, etc. It got in trouble when it assumed that hard work made the grade with St. Peter, the Gatekeeper of Heaven. St. Pete's got a book, and it isn't filled with Green Stamps.

It's filled with names. The names are of those that acknowledged that it isn't what you do, but who you know in life that gets you in to Heaven. Moralism is the cowpox, this time good, which prevented the best.

The maker and owner of all mankind laid down His standard for deciding who are His and who are not. The who that you need to know in life is Jesus Christ, and He must be known as Savior and Lord. That's how you get past St. Peter into blissful eternity. Otherwise you get eternity without the bliss.

The cowpox of humankind is the Great American Myth. If God is your copilot, swap seats.

Tell me what you think, I'm just thinkin out loud.

Its Not Our Thing

There have to be generations upon generations of people who think Jesus really blew it when He did not go immediately to the side of Lazarus to heal him when He heard Lazarus was ill. I mean look at it, the reputation of Jesus as healer. Surely He would scurry to the side of his friend to keep him out of the grave. But no, He didn't. He just went about business as usual and took care of Lazarus on His own time, in His own way. Lazarus died, but he walked again.

And then in Mark there was this time when, instead of a stroll around the Sea of Galilee, Jesus brings up the wise idea of a shortcut trip via boat. Jesus was quite tired, so he made like a Greyhound bus passenger, leaving the driving to others while He went to sleep in the back. He had said, "lets go to the other side". Well, that's ok, they thought so they took Him along in their boat and proceeded to cross the Sea. But there was a storm on the way, and it was like a hurricane. Wind was blowing, and the waves were crashing into the boat. Annoyed that their esteemed passenger was oblivious to all of this, they yelled at Jesus " Master don't you care that we are drowning?" Well, he took care of that situation, and then got upset with his disciples because, though they thought they knew who He was, they really didn't.

It is not up to us to tackle the issues of life with a plastic Jesus on the dashboard like he was a good luck charm or a magician. It is up to us to get to know Him like He really is, Lord of all. It's just our appointed duty to trust and obey what He says. We should keep it in mind that, even though we are going through the storms, he started us out on our own particular route saying, "Let us go to the other side". He always knew we'd get there.

Going where He says to go is our thing, getting us there is His.

Tell me what you think, I'm just thinkin out loud!

Between a Rock and a harder place

In the act of avoiding a revealed truth because it seems unbelievable, many people strike out in a similar, but seemingly <u>more</u> believable direction. The trouble is, the conclusion of this direction is a far <u>less</u> believable idea:

The young college student was sobbing as she walked into her pastor's study. She had had her faith put under attack, it seems.

Student: (between sobs) my professor laughed at me for believing the story of Moses and Israel's escape from Egypt.

Pastor: Oh! How so?

Student: He said the Israelis found a shallow place and waded across.

Pastor: Young lady, do you realize how fantastic and incredible a statement it is that you have just made?

Student: Well no, not really. I'm just telling you what he said.

Pastor: Well think of the inevitable next event: If the Israelis did find a shallow place and wade across the Red Sea, then an entire mounted Egyptian Army, chariots, horses and all, drowned in wading water! Now THAT is harder for me to believe than what is written in Scripture.

Steer clear of the Rock and you end up in a harder place!

Tell me what you think, I'm just thinkin out loud!

Out of Control!

Proverbs- Like a city broken into, and without walls is a man with no control over his spirit.

Pogo -We have met the enemy and he is us!

Phantom of the Opera- Masquerade! Paper faces on parade, Masquerade! Hide your faces so the world will never find you!

One of the most insightful aspects of any culture is its art! Artists tend to see it and say it like it is! Music, opera, comics they all have people who see society and its sham, it's out of control ways, its fear of being truly known. The expressions of man in his own world as he would have it show his desperate search for meaning and fulfillment. People want control of the world while they cannot even control themselves! The rock band Chicago recorded many a song of this sort. They noticed the attitudes of people around them, and sung about it all.

While most artists advance the philosophies of this world, some others have found an anchor, a place to steady themselves and be satisfied on a lasting basis. They see that the appetites of the soul are appetites that are never satisfied-doing, being and having.

The freedom of living is not unending freedom of gorging the soul, but rather of controlling it to keep it from self-destruction. People with no peace about themselves masquerade as something, somebody else, hoping no one will ever find them as they are.

There is someone who can love and satisfy people as no human can, but that someone requires self-control, obedience and trust. He does not require this without providing a means of doing it. His work in a soul goes out from the inside, providing first love, joy and peace and goes from there.

Self-Control- its there for the asking, but you'll never ask until you recognize and accept that you need it.

Tell me what you think, I'm just thinkin out loud!

Always In Control

Some people say that a proper way to see history is to just add an s to the word. This makes it hisstory, which doesn't make any sense until you separate the s's. Then you get an understanding of what's been going on all this time and who's behind it all.

There's a scene in the Gospels where Jesus says some things that get the Pharisees and priests all fired up, so they grab him and march Him up a hill to push Him off a cliff, but he disappears. He just vaporizes Himself because they'll do it better later anyway, and it's not time for that yet. Wonder how they explained his getting away that time?

Then later on, they really do have him, with a kiss of death to mark his identity, and rush right out. They break 11 of their laws and nail Him for sure, they think. But He didn't stay nailed, or dead. He not only rose from the dead, but also put on some traveling clothes somewhere along the line. I mean, who put the packed suitcase in the tomb with Him? None is mentioned.

So, before you try to figure out who did what and when, pay some serious attention to the first four words of Genesis . . . and go from there.

Tell me what you think, I'm just thinkin out loud!

It doesn't hurt to have heroes

You know, when you are driving down a road or heading in a direction and don't know what lies ahead, it sure helps to have help from someone or ones who has been there. These people may have responded to particular challenges in ways you may not have thought of. Their particular style and attitude may be an attraction to you.

Some people approach totally new opportunities with such a confidence that they almost make handling the situation look easy.
They serve as an inspiration and therefore deserve the title of "hero".
Orson Welles did this for me. He had never directed a movie before, but he had such confidence that he went and took his Mercury Radio Theater players and made them the characters in his first effort, "Citizen Kane". It is regarded as one of the best films ever made.

Memphian Kemmons Wilson went on a vacation with his family and the hotel costs so infuriated him that he started a chain of hotels that would suit him and, he thought, anybody else with a family the size of his. When he told his wife he would start a chain of hotels that would have 400 hotels, she laughed. Later on, so did he- all the way to the bank. But what makes him a hero is not just the determination to start and operate Holiday Inns, which he did. He is also great because all that money and fame did not change who he is. A wealth of money to him is not really a necessity. It's just a way of keeping score. He grew up as a humble, honest hard-working man and stayed that way to his grave. Wealth doesn't change people. It brings out who they are to begin with, given the means.

There have been a couple of musically talented people whose body of work I have always admired. One of them is Elton John. I may not agree with his lifestyle, but his musical genius is without peer to me. Another is Andrew Lloyd Webber, writer of music for such Broadway hits as "Cats" and "Phantom of the Opera". I hear their music in my head all the time.

I also draw a good deal of inspiration from David, Daniel and Joshua, in the Old Testament. Their verses would inspire anybody to move in faith.

Heroes give us good roadmaps to live and work by. We can't have too many.

Tell me what you think, I'm just thinkin out loud!

You can do this, but you can't do that!

One of the silliest ideas of all time is that one person could perform most any feat, master any skill. It sounds impressive for one person to say that, but it just is not true. No one person has the temperament, talent and energy to be able to do just anything and everything.

A great many people set out to master a number of different areas of expertise, excelling in a few, doing okay in others. Still others have a good idea of where their skills are focused. Some have not a clue. A smart surgeon pays no attention to the machinery of a woodworking shop. Knowing the danger of a slip, he keeps his fingers out of harm's way, in good working shape for more valuable talents and tasks. There are things you might try, but better not.

The truth named "great in some, okay in others" bore itself out well in the saga of Michael Jordan, the great NBA Basketball star. He left basketball to try his hand at pro baseball. He ended up in a minor league team, where he didn't stay. He decided the best use of his talent was where it was already evident, so he returned to basketball for a few more seasons of play before he retired.

It's no shame to realize what you should not be pursuing. It's only a shame not to find out and pursue what you might be good at.

Tell me what you think, I'm just thinkin out loud!

It's a Standing Arrangement

There are times in any believer's life when the pressures of living drive a person in directions that may not be the healthiest. These directions may come from before the person became a Christian, so they are old thought patterns, beliefs and behaviors. When this happens and the person sees himself or herself caught in a sin pattern, they become discouraged about themselves, and think they cannot get it turned around. But there is a hope to be considered.

One person who is struggling with a sin said they did not want to "bargain with God" to get His blessing. Thing is, they don't have to.

As it turns out God Himself struck a bargain with Israel in the Old Testament, and restated it many times in those pages. He told them: Walk with me, honor, trust and obey me, and I will bless you. Walk away and I will allow you to be overtaken by your enemies. He stuck with that arrangement completely and honored Israel's good behavior. He also stuck with it when Babylon burned the cities and hauled off the remnant. But what's important to remember is that the arrangement still exists between God and His people.

From the Old Testament to the New, one big change occurs here and that is the payment for sin, the means of satisfaction. Lambs and rams and other animals were replaced by one Person, Jesus Christ. The rest of the deal is still intact, and still honored by the original presenter of the deal, God Himself.

So, if you feel like you are stuck in a hole of sin but want to climb out, you don't have to "bargain with God". He's always presenting His bargain to you, just like He did to Israel. It's a standing arrangement.

Tell me what you think, I'm just thinkin out loud!

Wanna be an airplane?

Some people just carry an aura about them. When they are present in a place the sense is that someone really special is there.

Sometimes the reason they are special is that they have a title. Certain privileges and procedures accompany an officeholder, sometimes.

When a certain man was President of the U.S., the plane he flew in was called Air Force One. When he left office, and the same plane took him to a new home, the plane was called Special Mission One. Whatever airplane the president flies on is called Air Force One. It has that title because his presence is there.

Believers are special people. They have the title of God's own children, because he is "on board" them in their spirit. It is His Spirit that makes believers able to do His will, and marks them as His own.

Wanna be an airplane? Can't do it, but you can carry His Spirit. As many as receive Him to them He gives them the right to be called His Children.

Tell me what you think, I'm just thinkin out loud!

How would you handle it?

Matt got a phone at about 11:30 p.m. from a friend who woke him with bad news. The train their families were traveling on had been involved in an accident, and they had no idea how bad it was, or who was injured, etc. He quickly got dressed, joined his friend and they headed for the crash site, in Illinois, some 500 miles north.

While en route, Matt's wife, Cindy, called from her cell phone at the crash site. She said she had one of their three daughters with her, but was totally uncertain as to the fate of the two others. As it turned out, they had been in the club car with other young friends when the train hit a truck loaded with steel. The truck driver had no indication a train was coming, so he pulled his truck onto the tracks. The train hit the truck in the middle of the load, stopping a speeding passenger train from a high-speed cruise instantly. After that, the leaking diesel fuel caught fire, and burned the front two cars, including the club car, and all occupants.

Matt's first comment was that he felt they must "shepherd the tragedy" to make the most for God's Glory in the media. They did not want to sound bitter toward God, or the truck driver. Noting that, the press was absolutely amazed that anybody could lose children in a horrible, completely avoidable situation and not hate or be mad at somebody. A year later a network news correspondent was doing a follow-up story on the affected families. Matt and Cindy sounded the same then too.

Nothing but a sure and sound presence of the Holy Spirit can make that kind of response possible. No one can tell how he or she would respond; no one wants to be there. Its just one instance when God heads us toward extremely trying times when all we have is Him, but He's all we need.

Tell me what you think, I'm just thinkin out loud!

Be a Sputnik!

Sputnik Monroe took Memphis by storm in the 1950's. He was originally a carnival wrestler, and would wrestle anybody or anything to draw a crowd. From bears to other pro wrestlers, Sputnik had all manner of opponents, and he had a following. He also had a sense of right and wrong on some issues, and took on society with his brash, combative way.

The local laws forbade white people to walk on Beale St, an attempt to segregate the races; Sputnik walked down Beale St, and defied the law. He became a hero to Memphis' black community. They were his fans, not just because of his stand, but his brash ways in the wrestling ring. In the days of wrestling in Memphis's Ellis Auditorium, the promoters wanted to keep the races apart. They had the ushers count and admit only so many Negroes, whom they sat in the balcony. Sputnik knew about this, and, before the match, was in the lobby paying the ushers not to count. He packed the balconies. Just as Elvis Presley and Jerry Lee Lewis thought nothing of putting elements of black music into theirs, Sputnik integrated the wrestling ring. He had the same level of fame in wrestling that they had in music.

Once, in Mobile Alabama, a white woman saw him driving down a street with a black man in his car. She called him all manner of names, and ended up calling him a Sputnik. Americans in that day hated the Russians getting a space ship, Sputnik, into space ahead of them. In her anger the woman named him something she hated, for his flaunting of social order. He liked the name and kept it, Sputnik Monroe.

It takes people willing to be tough and willing to do what is right; to bring about what is good for the Kingdom of God. There is a sense of Spirit empowered ability to stand up to wrong attitudes and rules. It takes someone who knows his or her calling, and place (See Esther). It's not a humanly empowered strength; just ask King David and Gideon.

Sometimes ya just gotta be a Sputnik!

Tell me what you think, I'm just thinkin out loud!

Can't Stop the Itch!

Last weekend I paid a visit to the Yuppie's Toy Store, Sharper Image. They seem to have always more ingenious ways to separate young upwardly mobile adults from their cash bonuses. From skyscraper CD racks, to see through CD players that you can listen to in the shower, these people come up with newer and more eye-catching toys to trade for your cash.

Some of the more expensive toys are chairs that massage the back and feet. I saw two, of different prices for the more and less well heeled among us. They had back scratchers in different price ranges, too. Foot massagers, yeah they were there. Seems like a person with too much time and money could go broke and have a comfortable time doing it. But there are some itches we humans have that not even the Yuppie's Toy Store can scratch.

It doesn't have to be an image driven "keep up with the Joneses" complex that pushes us to have things. It's somehow that life itself is pretty empty without stuff. We all live for stuff, sometimes, whether its stuff to do, stuff to be, or stuff to have. That's an itch we don't know how to deal with, because most of the time we don't take care of it right.

We were born with it, and it never leaves us alone for long.

But the Creator God who built it into our nature has just such a way.

It's all answered in seeking Him to scratch that itch. When we approach Him and ask Him to deal with it, He does it. He gives us Himself. It isn't that the toys are bad, just that they won't scratch on a lasting basis. The bad things we are supposed to avoid aren't always so evil; they're just inadequate to the task of providing lasting satisfaction.

All those toys can scratch your back for a long time, but they can't always scratch your itch.

Tell me what you think, I'm just thinkin out loud!

Ya don't need to go there!

Most people know that as they travel high in the air, the air thins out and to breathe normally takes pressurized air. Airliners are designed to take care of this automatically with pressurization systems. Other types of aircraft use compressed air tanks. Water boils at a lower temperature at high altitudes because of lower air pressure.

Airliners commonly cruise in the lower 40,000's of feet for good fuel economy, but get it much over 45,000 feet and two situations develop from the thin air: the stall speed of the plane goes up and the speed of sound comes down. At 600 miles an hour a pilot can stall this heavily loaded airplane if he slows down very much, but if he speeds up, the plane shakes like a wet dog going through the speed of sound at that altitude.

So, too, there are places that God's people put themselves in a special peril in approaching. Horoscopes, tarot cards, ouija boards, the occult in general are part of the territorial province of the enemies of God. Whether or not the believer knows it, he or she is in serious danger in even appeasing a curiosity there. Seeking guidance of anyone besides

God Himself or His appointed agents comes under a Divine curse. God's people have no business seeking anyone but Him for guidance in life issues. Israel's first king, Saul, lost a great deal by having a sorcerer conjure up the spirit of the dead Samuel. Samuel's spirit did come up, and announced to Saul that God had decided to take his throne away from him.

Danger signs are a fair warning- don't ignore em'.

Tell me what you think, I'm just thinkin out loud!

The Talking Rock

Said the rock- It's so beautiful! Here I am, sitting on the shore at St. Andrews, Scotland. Children can play on me, grownups can lean on me, whole families can stand on me together for portraits!
Said the Maker- Yes, but I can make you even more beautiful.
Rock- Really ?? How?
Maker- I will send my North Sea crashing in on you for years and years. The wind, rain, and sand will wear you down. I will strike you with lightning, creating pockets on your surface. You will be so scarred that people will look at you and think that you are sand.
Rock- OUCH!!! Why so much <u>pain</u>?
Maker- I could not make you that beautiful any other way.

Jim Williams

© 2013 Jim Williams

The best laid plans

A family arrives at a beach and the youngsters unload the car like commandoes to battle positions. One of them, a boy, grabs his pail and shovel and heads off to the beach. Thinking he might be safer to do his work inland, he sets about piling sand some 10-15' in from the shore. He is going to build a sand chalet, a work of art, a place to behold. He piles up the sand and shapes it into a hill. He is going to make this pile of sand look like something any ant colony would be proud to call home.

He pays no attention to a group of clouds offshore that are gathering and looking darker all the time. The wind when he arrived was running across the beach, he'd checked. He felt safe, having built so far in from the waves and having a wind that seemed friendly to his plan at the time. But as clouds gather, they get bigger, as do the waves. Pretty soon the wind has shifted, blowing toward the shore off the water. The build-up of the waves is now catching his attention and he is getting worried, fearing the demise of all his efforts.

Finally his parents' call in all the children to leave the beach and the boy must leave his sand condo.

As he does, a huge wave rolls in and demolishes his afternoon's creative genius.

Some of us build our lives just like a kid with a sand castle. It maybe looks strong and beautiful, but one big event comes along and wipes it out.

We have our plans and sometimes they work, sometimes they don't. Sometimes the best thing that can happen is disaster. It has a way of opening a wise person's eyes. A wise person is one who asks God what He wants. An even wiser person asks that question before building the career. Proverbs 16:3 says that the mind of man plans his way, but the Lord directs His steps. The sovereignty of God makes this apply not only to believers but also to those who will become believers as a result of the tragedies in their lives.

Sometimes the worst that can happen- is actually the best!

Tell me what you think, I'm just thinkin out loud!

Don't miss a chance

Otis had just returned to Memphis from San Francisco where he'd sung a concert and written a song. He took the song to the studio where he recorded it. Toward the end, he whistled because he'd forgotten the words. He knew he had to re-record but would like to do it another day. He had a gig in Wisconsin and would do it when he got back. The producer said, "Okay, we'll do that".

But Otis' plane crashed into Lake Michigan on the way to the gig, and "Dock of the Bay" still has the whistle on the end. The producer had to scramble to put a recording together for the record label, but he did. Only the re-recording was lost to tragedy.

You never know when the last time is that you will see or talk to someone, usually. A football coach's widow said she heard a voice inside her tell, "you'll never see him again", as she looked at him one morning. He died in a plane crash that night.

My girlfriend has a very sweet habit of hugging both parents every time she leaves them. She lives with them and takes care of them, both in their 80's. You just never know which time is the last.

So take the chance to do what you can when you can.

The Whole World's Watching!

In 1968 there was a violent protest at the National Convention for the Democratic Party in Chicago. As protesters gathered and advanced, the onlookers and protesters both shouted, "The whole world's watching", while police lines advanced toward the protesters.

The protesters were pointing out that the gathered media was paying as much attention to the activities outside the convention hall as to the activities inside.

The city police of Chicago were put on notice that their reaction to the protest was as much a matter of importance as the protesters and their activities. What the protest was about was much more than the convention itself. It was about the way the country was being run, the war that the US was fighting at the time.

It is not too dissimilar a statement to say that the "Whole World's Watching" how we as God's people are living our lives. We have our issues much the same as the people who follow their own gods. How we react to those issues, deal with those conflicts, and carry on is either a source of encouragement or a point of hurt to the on looking world. Our influence is the most critical and crucial thing in this world. Will we lead and influence it, or let it lead and influence us?

Whatever we do, the whole world's watching.

Tell me what you think, I'm just thinkin out loud!

Don't go too far!

Barge piloting has never been an easy career choice, what with the body of water you are navigating on constantly changing direction and course. Writer Mark Twain made a life on boats up and down the Mississippi River, learning every turn, every nuance that the river came up with to challenge the mettle of steamboat captains. The name Mark Twain is a river term having to do with water depth.

It's not much different now, really. With a high and low level over 40 feet apart over a year's time, its always interesting where the river is gonna go now. One technique for approaching turns was shared with me by a late riverboat captain, Jake Meanley. As a tug approaches the turn in the river south of Memphis for example, going downstream, he has his rudders turned into the turn, engines at hard reverse. Jake said that if a boat came thru the turn not set that way, it was a good possibility the back of the whole barge-tug configuration, the tug, would fan out toward the outer bank of the turn, turning completely sideways to the current. This is called flanking; some may also call it fishtailing. Using brakes going in is a good way of showing restraint in the process of a good activity, keeping it from going bad, by regulating its natural forces involved.

There are some activities human beings get involved in as a natural course of living that need some restraint to keep a good thing from leading to a bad one. Eating is a good example, but really this can involve any appetite. The appetites are there for survival, but the overdone indulgence can defeat the purpose of the appetite.

Barges have to make turns to stay in the river channel; we have to eat to stay alive. But in both cases without restraint, there can be a disaster. It takes brakes to do it right.

Watch your turns, watch your intake.

Tell me what you think, I'm just thinkin out loud!

Watch em fall!

When Israel was cruisin right along, they apparently thought they could do no wrong. Just go to war, take along the Ark of the Covenant, like a Divine rabbit's foot, and "the battle am in my hand". Well, one time they tried that trick, and got their clocks cleaned, their bells rung, and just plain lost the battle. Not only that, they lost the Ark, too. The Philistines figured this was one neat toy, this ark. They must have said to each other, nodding agreement, "Israel's been standing on our necks long enough with this thing. Now it's our turn!"

The first thing they did was to introduce Israel's God to their own god, Dagon. They parked the Ark of the Covenant in the same room with the statue of Dagon. Come next morning, Dagon's on the floor, on his face before the ark. Well, they didn't feel any earthquake the night before, so they didn't know what happened. So they put Dagon back up in his place. The next morning, same thing, only now he is torso only. The head, and all arms and legs were broken off. Dagon disintegrated like idols do.

When two planes went crashing into the two New York buildings, the icons of American economic strength, they weren't the only gods that fell. In the face of this assault, Americans became less trustful in the same old things that had brought them such a comfortable lifestyle. Out came the nationalism, and out came the prayer books, church clothes and words of prayer were heard a lot more often. Sales of Gospel music have skyrocketed since then.

People have their gods that they trust to serve and protect them and their way of life. But let those gods be attacked, and people know they have only one God to depend on. All those idols of living and pleasure go by the wayside when its time to really lean on someone to protect them. Even that broadcast agnostic, NBC's Katie Couric, who regularly roasted Christians on national TV, was heard saying equally regularly "we will pray".

We had our smugness, and we have our gods, but when the chips are down, watch em fall!

Tell me what you think, I'm just thinkin out loud!

A Pictorial Penalty

If history has anything it has lessons that only wise people ever learn. The fools ignore and refuse to accept the manner of the penalties meted out, and the penalties end up matching the sins. Don't think so? Go look at the plagues of Egypt when Moses told Pharaoh "let my people go!" Nearly every one of them involved a mockery of an Egyptian god.

The massive loss of human life in New York and Washington on 9/11/2001 pales in comparison to what has happened in American abortion clinics for the past 28 years. A nation which holds the value of human life in such low esteem now faces a foe which has an equal disregard for guess what-human life, including their own.

If you refuse any spiritual significance to the events of September 11, 2001, then don't be surprised when history clears its throat with a suicide bomber in your malls and public gatherings.

If you wave your flags in pride and ignore any notion of your own sins, history will hiccup in your face. It happened to Israel, and it's coming to a crowd near you.

Don't ignore the overwhelming disregard and masterful execution of human life in New York, Washington and your local abortion clinics. It cannot be escaped anymore.

Tell me what you think, I'm just thinkin out loud! And I wonder who, if anybody, is listening!

Yeah, but there's four of em'

Just ahead of a football game between the University of Tennessee and then Memphis State a Memphis State fan made a comment to the Tennessee broadcast sports announcer. He told the man that his team would do well in the first quarter of the game. The announcer reminded him "yeah, but there's four of em".

In the face of all that is going on the world now, with persecution, prosecutions and other bad happenings, it is so important to remember that the Creator, God, is not surprised. He allowed and had His purposes in the happenings of September 11, 2001.

The terrorists are going to exact their deeds on the US and its allies, but not all that are planned. Not only that, they don't have the last say. Read in the early chapters of Job and you will see that Satan can only do what he is allowed to.

So go read the headlines, but remember that the end of those stories is already in the book of Revelation.

The Devil appears to get ahead sometimes, but, these days, it's just the first quarter, and there's four of em'.

Tell me what you think, I'm just thinkin out loud.

In Search of Irrational Peace

Sometimes the pain of a worry is worse than the cause of it. The thing bothering us can be less than the pain it causes. This is true, usually because there are other worries associated with it, and they add to the emotional weight of the misery.

Sometimes the company, which is contracted to pick up and empty the huge trashcans across the street from me, comes at an early hour. Its always the same- the truck comes, picks up the can, throws it over the cab, tips it over and empties it into his bin. Then he puts the container down and drives off with the trash.

The pain of our worries is something God wants to come pick up and take off our hearts, just like the truck empties the cans. The very glaring difference here is the peace we have when the troubles are carried off. We have peace. It doesn't make sense to our thinking, because we might not immediately have the answers we want. But we have the peace. The peace doesn't make sense, but it makes us calm inside.

Philippians 4:7 speaks to the anxiety surrounding a worry. The previous verse has already encouraged us to hand the worry over to God. Then comes the promise of the peace that passes understanding- the irrational peace. It doesn't go directly opposite the worry; it goes above it, like an upper level wind.

Prayer over a problem approaches God. He lifts us out of it and into an upper level of peace. Its not against reason, it's above it.

Tell me what you think, I'm just thinkin out loud!

Take no prisoners!

It was a cool sunny April morning when a group of rebel soldiers set out northward from Corinth, Mississippi in search of northern encampments. It did not take them long to find one after they got into Tennessee. Well armed and supplied, they shot and shot until they pinned the yankees down behind a place called the Hornet's Nest. As evening approached, the confederate soldiers laid down their weapons without vanquishing entirely the remaining soldiers.

After darkness set in, the yankee general brought in reinforcements and lobbed cannon balls at the rebels during the night to prevent them getting sleep. The next day the Yankee forces, fresh soldiers added, pushed back the attackers clear out of the battlefield.

Thus was the Battle of Shiloh, early in the US Civil War.

How many times do we face an enemy and push it back, but let it stay the night with us? The Confederate States of America lost a battle they could have won had they wiped out the resistance the first day. They thought they could afford to take it up the next day, having holed them up beside the Tennessee River.

Something that can destroy you cannot be allowed to stay near you. It has to be virtually wiped out at the moment of encounter.

Tell me what you think, I'm just thinkin out loud!

The constant present tense

In this world, we speak of people, places and events that are, have been and will be. People come and go, events happen, and places exist and some cease to exist. All three tenses come into play in the description of creation.

But when it comes to the Creator, God, only one tense fits. Sometimes, for support of our faith, we speak of something He did in the past tense, but that is an event, part of creation. The person of God is always only in the present tense. We have no reference to Him any other way in terms of time. We create idols and they have a beginning of our making, but the one true God was never created.

A very sarcastic film by James Broughton seeks to refute the existence of God by starting off with the line "in the beginning, it was already there". As a created evidence of His presence, it was not, but He was. What the film tries to say is creation always existed, which is an absurdity. Creation got created at some point, but when and by whom? Its not creation otherwise, it's God Himself and He is not His creation. Created beings by definition cannot create themselves.

The God who spoke to Moses called Himself "I Am". What utter unmitigated gall! Unless it's really true! Natural man would call that name a statement of egotism gone mad, because his mind cannot conceive the Creator as He is. It takes a step of acceptance and faith for the mind of man to conceive a being bigger than he is. God has to impart Himself in some form to such a limited mental capacity to get it to accept the larger reality.

Toward the end of the year, some men celebrate that imparting of God to men, allowing them to accept Him and receive Him as their God. We call that celebration Christmas!

The God who is, is there for us.

Tell me what you think, I'm just thinkin out loud!

Things we need-but don't know it!

The young band members had come to near the end of a recording session, but needed one more song to fill up the album they were recording. They ended up recording a song they really did not plan to include, one they sang at wedding receptions and other gigs. It ended up that the song was a hit. Using the mute guitar as lead instrument, "Mrs. Brown, you've got a lovely daughter" made Herman's Hermits an overnight sensation in March 1965.

Funny how sometimes in our lives we put in all the best stuff, all the most desirable elements. We leave out what we consider to be things we don't always use, just do for show. But it often turns out that all this stuff just aint enough! It so often feels like the words of that old Rolling Stones song," Satisfaction".

Somehow we have to look at ourselves and consider that something else could be just as good as what we have- or better. It takes a leap of faith to think that a move that seems unfamiliar or in some ways unattractive could be a good direction for us. In fact it might be a hit for us. Somehow we have to do something about the emptiness inside, but the options are not particularly attractive sometimes.

Jeremiah 29:11 means what it says-check it out.

Tell me what you think, I'm just thinkin out loud!

The Grenade Jumper

The movie "M*A*S*H" was a tremendous success when it hit the silver screen in 1970. It was such a good situation, material for lots of entertainment, that it spawned a TV series, just as some earlier WWII movies had. The TV series MASH ran for 11 years, and had a character carried over from the movie with the same actor playing it.

In one episode of the TV series, the doctors examined the newly arrived wounded soldiers. It was determined that one soldier was so badly injured that he was soon to die. Having decided this, the doctors decided one of his organs could be put in the body of another soldier who needed that organ. A third soldier heard this conversation and protested loudly.

The surgeries went just as planned, and the living soldier was given the dying soldier's organ. Then the chaplain visited the third soldier concerning his complaint. He said that the dying soldier, a commanding officer in his unit, sounded like the type who would dive on a grenade, and give up his life to save the other soldiers in his unit. The soldier said, " yes, he would." The chaplain then said, "he just did".

Jesus jumped on a grenade for you. What are you gonna do about it?

Tell me what you think, I'm just thinkin out loud!

Who are the heroes?

When jets hit buildings and people started getting out of the buildings and areas as fast as they could, there were people, some off-duty, who rushed toward the calamity. A great many of those were killed when the buildings they occupied collapsed in on them. For their show of daring they were called heroes. Heroes they were, indeed.

When it comes to walking toward the fray, though, another kind of hero also emerges, but it's a different kind of fray. There is a spiritual battleground, an unseen warfare for which a different kind of soldier is created. In John 17, Jesus spoke of His servants and the conditions surroundings them. Jesus says, in a prayer " as you sent me into the world, so I have sent them into the world".

So the people called by God's name are called as lifesavers, as warriors, going toward the fray from which people seek a release and relief everyday. Life itself is a situation where there are forces at battle for souls. Before you read the middle passages of history, go to the end of Scripture and you will see- the heroes win!

Jesus told Peter that he held the keys to heaven. He also said that the gates of hell would not prevail against the spread of His word. Gates are defensive devices, designed to hold the captives in. The heroes are to storm those gates and rescue those caught in the strongholds.

The people in fireman's suits and police uniforms saving people from burning buildings and terrorists are the world's heroes. The people in plain clothes saving people from the cost of their own sin are heaven's.

Tell me what you think, I'm just thinkin out loud!

Places you have to go

Interstate Highway 15 goes through the Mojave Desert for a long stretch, namely from the Los Angeles area to Las Vegas Nevada, and beyond. A drive up or down this road takes a tank full of gas and a heart full of patience. I have driven it a few times in past days and find it interesting and boring at the same time.

Western US visibility is in the 100-mile range commonly. Traveling up and down the hills of the Mojave is a long drawn out experience, especially if you are used to driving in the eastern US where hills are short and visibility a few miles. Drive I-15 in either direction from LA to Vegas and you are going to go up a hill for 20 minutes, then down to a valley for another 20 minutes. You spend close to an hour getting past some hills because they are very large and very far away. Your eyes play tricks on you when you are used to passing a hill and getting on. Add to all of this a sometimes-high windstorm that can take all the paint off a car with the fine Mojave sand.

Sometimes the path of our lives can be like this desert trek. We go through a long uphill stretch and feel good about it because a high point is a high point. Feelings are good and usually so are circumstances.

But getting to the next high point calls for going down first and for a long time. And just like the far off hills we don't have to cross, but would like to pass and go on to something else, there are people and situations in our lives that we wish would just get on and get away from us. We want always to be headed upwards, going toward a positive place. The valleys we not only have to go through, but deal with on an extended, time consuming basis. Physical pain comes to mind, maybe disease. Maybe its something we get into because we hate some thing we want to avoid for ourselves or someone else close to us. It is also true how God refines us in these times. The words of the song "How firm a foundation" come to mind with the end words of a verse- *thy dross to consume and thy gold to refine.* It takes the hard parts of living to clean the junk off the good parts of us.

The low points of living become the high points of life!

Tell me what you think, I'm just thinkin out loud!

Who's got who?

The Gospel of John provides an interesting glimpse into the arrest of Jesus by the authorities. John told his own version of the events, leaving out details that others included. His story telling almost made me wonder, "who's arresting who?"

Look at John, chapter 18, v1-8. Jesus was standing there in an olive grove with friends and along came some Roman soldiers and church officials. Jesus approached them and asked them "who is it you want?" "Jesus of Nazareth" they said. "I Am," he said. ("he" is added by translators). On hearing this, they all fell to the ground! So here we are, Jesus is standing up, and they are on their faces. Who's arresting who?

These were the folks who had come to arrest Jesus, to carry on their kangaroo court and hang Him on a cross, as if THEY were in charge. But what was the first thing they did when confronted with Him, in His holiness? When Jesus got <u>in</u> their faces, they got <u>on</u> em'

These so-called best-laid plans of mice and men weren't laid by mice or men. Guess who did make 'em? And why? The answers may change your life.

Tell me what you think, I'm just thinkin out loud!

Break down those Walls!

The deification of man in modern culture shows itself best in a song called "The Wall", by the rock group Pink Floyd. In their view, man at any age and stage is fit for heaven and earth without any need for "thought control". A baby should not be turned away from touching a hot stove, as such a warning would be "thought control" according to this kind of thinking.

Problem is, man didn't make creation. God did, and He designed the physical universe whose laws made possible the recording of their song. But how is it evident that God, any god, made anything, that creation didn't happen without being a Divine idea in the first place? Looking at creation soon turns to looking at its design, and in this process it becomes evident that there is a sense of order. Certain ideas and objects came to be because certain other ideas and objects preceded them. Seeds in the ground lead to seedlings above the ground, leading to buds, leading to plants, flowers, etc. Creation advertises its own sense of order by its very existence!

The discovery of the order of creation is the idea behind education. People can share ideas with other people, and thereby enhance their lives in sharing.

This isn't "thought control", as Pink Floyd puts it but it is thought nurturing. As the communist party found out in their indoctrination exercises in the early 20th century, peoples' minds cannot truly be controlled. Through one incentive or motivation or another, the human mind can only be encouraged in one direction or another. There is no such thing as thought control because one person can never have that power over another.

The collection of paper and ink called the Holy Bible is a totally unique one in that it has the endorsement and enforcement of its ideas in human hearts by its original speaker, God Himself. That again is not thought control, but rather thought nurturing. It teaches, in the same way in which books about natural law do, that there are laws, choices and consequences. Be it near or far, there will always be a payday someday.

We're not just another brick in the wall; we're building blocks in God's Creation!

Tell me what you think, I'm just thinkin out loud!

Isn't that enough?

The track runner makes a running approach and leaps 18 feet in a sand pit. How'd the judges know he'd jumped 18 feet? They measured the distance from where he left the ground to where he landed. By what standard was it measured? Who created it? Why is it accepted as a standard?

No measure of any effort, length, or anything else means anything unless it has wide acceptance. That standard has to be practically useful for all. The calendar we use today came about by trial and error. A year didn't come to be accepted at its current measure until it proved to be accurate relative to the movement of the earth around the sun. Aha! A standard set by a Divinely appointed event was a concept that became accepted by all. Man didn't measure rightly until he measured by God's appointed standards. He never does.

The wickedest days in the history of Israel were during the period of the Judges. "Every man did according to what was right in his own eyes," Scripture reads. When man sets the standards for living he sets up situational ethics, because not every man will accept the standards of another. But when every person accepts and adheres to the standards set by God, he has a universal measure to live by.

Heaven is God's city, His real estate, so He sets the standard for how to get in it. The Virgin Birth, sinless life and sacrificial death of His own Son satisfy Him as a standard. All a person has to do is accept them for him or herself and they get in. The Father set the standard and the Son met it. That's enough for God. Isn't that enough for you?

Tell me what you think, I'm just thinkin out loud!

The Impossible Infinite

Look up into the sky and try to imagine that of all the stars and darkness you can see, you can't see it all. The telescope flying around in space cannot see it all. That's because there's no end to it. Infinity is something we human beings cannot grasp.

We chart the skies, and we chart time, all in a vain effort to grasp the unending natures of time and space. But they do not lend themselves to being measured very far. Even the scientists who measure the universe say it's expanding. What's it expanding to? Where's it going?

It takes an effort to accept a Being who is also infinite in order to accept an infinite creation. That's something the mind has a hard time doing, because most people live as if there is nothing or no one, greater than himself or herself. But what if there is? It is a serious flaw in thought not to allow at least that possibility. Take that thought further to expand the greater Being and allow His possibility as a God who created everything and everyone and loves it all.

"If you believe in forever, then life is just a one night's stand", the song goes. What are you gonna do in your one night's stand?

Tell me what you think, I'm just thinkin out loud!

A Workable Solution

Infinity may be impossible to comprehend, but an infinite Being need not be. It is an affront to human pride to acknowledge any need of such a being, but laws are laws. Step off a building ledge at 10 stories and you are history regardless of what you believe about gravity. Die without a Savior and you're lost regardless of what you think about religion.

The act of saying that there is a God who is greater than all humanity is a big step, but a very important one. It's important not just to make dying bearable, but also to make living tolerable. The human race is a big herd of sheep, basically stupid and headed toward whatever latest fad grabs its fancy. It needs a maker to give its existence some good reason for being.

Thinking with a larger Being in mind gives the purpose of wondering how to find that Being and how to interact with it, or Him. This is called presuppositional thinking, because you set up the premise at first that there is a Being greater than yourself in existence. From there you go to getting to know this Being and interacting with it.

If you are truly open to this thinking, you will get where you are headed. "You will seek me and find me when you seek me with all your heart". That is the promise of Jeremiah 29:13. Think and seek-and find!

Tell me what you think, I'm just thinkin out loud!

Consider the Alternatives

It is profound to consider that there may be a God, and that He can be found when earnestly searched after. But some people instantly dismiss such an idea as a waste of time. They look anywhere and everywhere else for an idea to live by.

Consider one idea claimed by the convicted Oklahoma City bomber Timothy McVeigh. He cited a poem by Invictus as his last words. The idea goes like this "I am the captain of my fate, and the master of my destiny". Where it means that a person has sole responsibility for his decisions, this is true. The problem is that most people deny the consequences of those decisions. The possibility always exists that there could be a consequence of actions that is detrimental to perpetrator of the action. The laws of physics dictate the absolute nature of physical consequences. But what the poem denies is that there are any laws of God, because it implicitly denies Him. Spiritual consequences are something it would be wise to allow for.

That phrase also suggests the idea that a person has control of circumstances, which is absolute absurdity. It would further suggest that man has control of his eternal fate. How is a person a master of his fate? Where does the destiny end? Or does it? The term "master" has a sovereign ring to it. Who really is the master?

The phrase "master of my fate, captain of my destiny" has a ring of truth, but it assumes too much and does not answer enough questions about life. There are just too many negative possibilities attached, and no guarantee of a positive outcome, the supposed reward of such a philosophy.

Tell me what you think, I'm just thinkin out loud!

The Appetite for the Infinite

Did you ever wonder what would satisfy your biggest appetite? Did you want it so much, but did not have the means to have it? It's really scary what we would do if we could really get enough of what our appetites crave.

Imagine, if you can, that all mankind has a parent. Then try to believe that this parent didn't just impregnate someone who conceived a baby human being. He created the earth, and after a few days of setting up an environment, made a human. He then proceeded to pour out love on that human. When the human rejected him, he continued to pursue that person like a relentless lover, and continues the pursuit to this day. I'm speaking of it as absolute truth, but it's an idea to try out in your mind and see what life could be like if this idea was true for you. After all, you can't knock what you haven't really tried.

Now try this: Those cravings I mentioned starting out are interesting. None of them can be satisfied with earthly delights on a continuing basis. It takes an endless supply of things, activities and status to try to satisfy the human soul. Nothing on earth can satisfy this insatiable human appetite for the infinite. Only this parent that made it all can hit that deep, deep spot in the human soul.

It takes an infinite being to satisfy an infinite appetite.

Tell me what you think, I'm just thinkin out loud!

It's easy if you try

The man who caused the explosion that blew down a government building in the US died with these words:" I am master of my fate and captain of my destiny". He ran his own life and ended the lives of so many more. Another man faced the end of his life and his words affect so many millions of people via TV. Whenever TV networks run some bit of profound programming, they always throw in the John Lennon song "Imagine".

People make such gods of themselves with thoughts like "imagine there's no heaven, it's easy if you try, no hell below us, above us only sky". Sounds a bit like Isaiah 14: 14 where Satan is quoted- "I will be like the most High". When you refuse to accept the reality of God and his Sovereignty, there is no end to what you can dream up. Lennon is right on the mark here- it is easy if you try.

The pen is mightier than the sword, and the TV camera more devastating than the smart bomb. What we think and lead others to feel or think are crucial because we are all shepherds of sorts to our own bands of sheep. What we accept and declare to others has unfathomable effect on others. God's reality is there, and doesn't need imagining, just reading and accepting.

"You may say I'm the dreamer, but I'm not the only one". He's right; he's not the only one. Straight is the gate and narrow the way that leads to eternal life. All human life is eternal, it's just not considered to be life, if it is outside of Heaven.

If you don't want to accept God's laws for His creation, both physical and spiritual then imagine what you do want. Accept what is or imagine what isn't. Its easy if you try.

Tell me what you think, I'm just thinkin out loud!

Just leave it alone!

When I was in high school, there was a rumor going around the country that one of the Beatles, a rock group, was dead. Coming from Norse legends and other tales, the rumor-mongers were trying to convince people that Paul McCartney was dead. They pointed to "evidence" such as Paul walking across the street barefoot in an album cover picture when all the others walking with him had shoes on. This was consistent with one custom or another. The Beatles themselves admitted later on that they had no idea where their fans were coming from, dreaming up those stories.

The rumor-mongers evidently approached certain bodies of information with an emotionally strongly held idea, and found support. The fact is, anytime that a person approaches a body of information with a strongly held belief he/she will always find support for the belief. The heart will force an interpretation to suit its desire.

As it was with the Beatles, so it is with Scripture. It does not often render itself subject to interpretations. It mainly can be read, and The Holy Spirit relied upon to help you to understand it correctly. Just leave it alone and read it, knowing that it takes reading as a body of verses, some easier to understand verses, which help to explain certain hard to understand sections.

The Bible is not just a collection of ink and paper like any other text. It is a collection of verses, which are endorsed and convicted by God's Holy Spirit. He is the author and enforcer of the truth therein. No other book has that endorsement except as it repeats the truth originally spoken in Scripture.

You can interpret yourself into Hell. Just read and believe what's in the Scripture. Just leave it alone.

Tell me what you think, I'm just thinkin out loud.

Walkin on the water

He's got the whole world in His hands
He's got the whole world in His hands
He's got the whole world in His hands
He's got the whole world in His hands

He's got Ahmadinejad in His hands
He's got Al Qaeda and the Taliban in His hands
He's got Reid and Pelosi in His hands
He's got the whole world in His hands

He's got Republicans and Democrats in His hands
He's got Mitt Romney and Obama in His hands
He's got the U.S. Senate in His hands
He's got the whole world in His hands

He's got the corporation scandals in His hands
He's got the 401K's in His hands
He's got early forced retirement in His hands
He's got the whole world in His hands

He's got smart bombs and dirty bombs in His Hands
He's got car bombs and pipe bombs in His hands
He's got airplanes and snipers in His hands

He's got the whole world in His hands

He's Chapter 11 bankruptcy in His hands
He's got foreclosures and shutdowns in His hands
He's got your personal fortunes in His hands
He's got the whole world in His hands

God's present purpose is to enable you to see that He is walking on top of the affairs of your life just now.

Tell me what you think, I'm just thinkin out loud!

The trouble with 99.9%

This world prides itself on being *nearly* perfect. But it's not quite the cigar award level, actually. At a 99.9% performance level-

City water systems turn out one hour's worth of unsafe drinking water/ month.

There are two unsafe landings at Chicago's O'Hare Airport every day.

500 incorrect surgical procedures are performed each week.

16,000 pieces of mail get lost each hour

19,000 babies get dropped at birth each year

20,000 incorrect prescriptions are written and filled each year

22,000 checks get drawn on a wrong account each year

and

32,000 heartbeats are missed each year.

God's standard is perfection. He knows his creatures couldn't help the inadequacies of 99.9%, so He did something about it. He caused a woman to give birth to Someone who did live perfectly, and died sacrificially, so 99.9% didn't matter. We could all trade our 99.9% imperfection in for His 100% and get the cigar- and heaven.

99.9%- we don't have to settle for it- but we do have to trade it in.

Tell me what you think, I'm just thinkin out loud!

Everybody needs a Sam!

Recently, as yet another Sun Studios singing icon died, it was repeated that Sun's founder, Sam Phillips, was the one who made them famous. It was Sam's style to "give shy people . . . a voice."

Sam Phillips took the likes of people who were shy, insecure nobodies with a talent and made them big names like Johnny Cash, Carl Perkins, Roy Orbison, and that special kid from the housing project, Elvis Presley. Sam saw their gift, made them see it, believe in it and, as the late Johnny Cash put it, "taught me the importance of being an individual."

Wow! All those people were talented individuals, and in to their lives came someone who got to know them, saw their gift and encouraged them to develop it. He insisted on the vision he saw for them. When Johnny Cash lost a record of one of his songs, he went back to Sam, hoping to get another copy. Sam had a box with 24 other copies of that song. The copies were to be sent to radio stations all over the Southern US. Johnny told Sam "I won't be singing in all those cities". Sam told Johnny "Yes, you will". Johnny did sing in all those places, and more besides. Now he sings in Heaven.

We all need a Sam Phillips in our lives, someone who sees in us a glimmer of hope, a vision for how beautiful our lives can be. We can actually have that in a relationship with the Son of God. He knows us better than we know ourselves, won't sell us short and won't let us sell ourselves short, either. He can be truly the "friend who sticks closer than a brother".

Everybody needs a Sam, 'cause everybody needs a Savior!

Tell me what you think, I'm just thinkin' out loud.

The Ultimate Mousetrap

"Build a better mousetrap," an old saying goes, "and the world will beat a path to your door". Problem is, if the next mousetrap after yours is similar but inferior but gets better marketing, your mousetrap may soon lose its market and sales may go flat.

God had a plan for His creation to keep it close to Himself, but gave it self-will so it would come to Him out of choice, not robotic command. He offered it a host of pleasing, gratifying choices of things to consume, but a third party intervened and offered what looked like better marketing. The item offered was put forward with a lie, and a question as to the unavailability of the item considered.

God came back around with another item, a person, and He got competed with. The Third Party came up with all kinds of questions and lies about this person, and whether He was who He said He was. Once again, the second mousetrap got more attractive marketing, but some came to see that the original offering was indeed better.

False religion has always come on with questions about Jesus, and denials of His Deity. But in the end they have not been able to satisfy the longings of the heart of man on a continuing basis. The ultimate solution to the problems of mankind and the ultimate answer to the appetites of mankind have always been met in the offerings of the Creator of mankind.

Jesus is like the ultimate mousetrap.

Tell me what you think, I'm just thinkin out loud!

Three Voracious Drives

Ever wonder what satisfies the human soul-on a lasting basis? Ever consider what it would take to be at peace with your heart and stay that way in an ongoing style? We humans have three basic drives that know no satisfaction in this world. These drives are doing, having and being.

We have to do whatever our chief addiction says to. Our chief addiction is whatever experience tells us we are most satisfied to do. It can be money, sex, drugs, gambling, racing, etc. But whatever it is, NOTHING in this world will hit the spot on a lasting basis. We can earn money, have pleasure, do drugs, go to the casinos, drive cars or whatever fast or look at it happening- and still feel empty inside. It's like throwing a penny into the Grand Canyon.

We can have the big house, the attractive successful spouse, the chic car, the nicest, smartest kids- and what's it all for? When does it come to having enough to feel good about?

We can be the richest, most successful, most whatever that we want to be and so what?

King Solomon had all that. He did the doing, was the richest of any ruler before or since his time, and had it all. But in Ecclesiastes 2:11 he had to admit that it just meant nothing. He uses the phrase "chasing after the wind". It's as if he had been pursuing something he knew he could never catch and hold.

Temptation is the opportunity to have illegitimate satisfaction of a legitimate desire. Whoah! Were we built with this package of drives that cannot be satisfied? No! We were built with this package of drives that cannot be satisfied *in this world*! Solomon uses the phrase "under the sun". Above the sun, above it all, the Creator, God, built this voracious group of desires to get us to seek Him, because only He can satisfy them to the fullest, most peaceful extent.

The three voracious drives are like anything else in our lives that brings stress to us- they were meant to drive us to seek the author of life that He would take care of it all. It's God drawing us to Himself.

So take this stuff and shove it-into your prayer closet!

Tell me what you think, I'm just thinkin out loud!

Living in the Eye

The US government publishes a list of hurricane classes called the Saffir-Simpson Hurricane Scale. On this list it classes hurricanes by wind speed, and gives you an idea of what kind of damage to expect with each class. Class I Hurricanes can do much to scare you, with some coastal flooding, and it can do major damage to low-lying shores. Class V Hurricanes, however, command some real respect, though, with very high winds causing even greater damage. You can expect roof failures on residences and industrial buildings. Lower floors get completely flooded.

The hurricane has a place of peace though. Right in the middle of all this swirling wind is a calm place that has a real sense of security to it. It's called the eye. In the eye the hurricane that's tearing up your home is acting more like a nice day at the beach. You are guarded as long as you stay in the eye.

So how to stay in the eye in the storms of your life? Hezekiah knew how. When the commander of the Syrian forces came calling with a big army and an even bigger mouth that taunted Hezekiah, he knew which OP to go to. OP can be Outright Panic or Outpoured Prayer. Hezekiah poured out his heart, and Sennacherib got sent to the Loudmouth Hall of Shame. Hezekiah knew his God was even bigger than Sennacherib's mouth, and that He is Almighty to save when called on to do so.

Philippians Chapter 4, verse 6 tells us not to worry, but to pray. Verse 7 promises a reward for that prayer. It promises a peace that guards the heart and mind. A principle comes from this- God takes the storm out of us BEFORE He takes us out of the storm! This promised peace guards our hearts *and* minds, so we can live in the eye of all of our storms.

It's an ignorant bliss, this peace. We don't have any idea how God is going to fix our problems, just that He will.

Hurricanes move, though and take their eyes with 'em. As we pray and get in this eye, we will find ourselves drawn closer to our God by ever higher winds and more threatening circumstances. They will always escalate, because He will always use them to draw us closer and closer to Him, calling us away from all our worldly care. It takes a growing prayer life to stay in the eye, but it's the only way to be and stay there. Living in the eye is the only place to be!

Tell me what you think, I'm just thinkin out loud!

That Little Somethin Extra!

The rock band was in the recording studio to make an album. They needed 12 songs to complete, and had 11 of them down on tape. They scratched their heads, thought about it, and decided to use a piece they often performed at wedding receptions to complete the session. Not that they thought much of it, but it completed the job. "Mrs. Brown You've Got a Lovely Daughter" put Herman's Hermits on the charts as their first big hit, with that funky mute guitar sound. There was something they needed that they didn't think much of but it made the difference between early failure and success!

The rhythm and blues band just finished a very first song, but didn't like it. They asked the studio owner to name something that stunk. "Green Onions stink", she said, so they named it Green Onions, and it took them by surprise, jetting up the sales charts, and making Booker T & the MG's a household name. There was something they did well, but didn't like at all, but it made the difference in their lives, gaining them the recognition they sought as an instrumental bad.

2000 years ago, someone came into history and made himself an object of hatred to some, showing their hypocrisy, and to all, their need of Him. Some people don't think much of Him, some outright don't like Him, but to those who receive Him He turns, and continues to turn, their lives into something worth living! It only takes a try to see what Jesus can do for a soul, turning an existence into an abundant life! He stands outside the heart, knocking at the door, asking to come in.

What the two bands did with a song, you can do with a Person, and it will make all the difference in the world!

Tell me what you think, I'm just thinkin out loud!

Changing Directions

Sometimes we humans who have a Savior we know seldom give much attention to circumstances we don't like. Things happen, or don't happen, and we curse the happening or failure. We curse it because it stands in the way of doing what *we* want to do with our lives, and ourselves.

I love wedding photography. I don't do a very expensive job of it, because I don't have the wisdom or equipment for it. So when an email attachment of wedding pictures I was trying to send didn't load and go like I wanted, I was furious. But later, when I lost another lead to shoot a wedding, I stood back and wondered why. A famous preacher, Adrian Rogers, once said "God knocks by circumstances, and speaks by His Word". I quit shooting weddings.

When things don't go the way I think they should once, I might write it off as demonic interference. But when a pattern begins to show itself, I begin to consider the sovereignty of God and if He might be putting His foot on my path to change it. Sovereignty and patience mark His ways in our lives. Sovereignty, patience and encouragement in a new direction, or an old one I neglected because it meant doing things against my nature-like trusting Him for all my needs. I give lip service to faith, but what I really want to do is be self-sufficient in all ways. Such humanness stands as an explanation for some difficulties in my life sometimes. Being married and letting a mate be an avenue of provision when I was single for nearly 52 years is tough. I want to "show her". God wants to *use* her to lead me, to bless me, sometimes.

Proverbs 16:9 says "the mind of man plans his way, but the Lord directs his steps". So true; it's just a matter of how much directing He has to do before I wise up, see His path and follow Him in it.

Tell me what you think, I'm just thinkin out loud.

Its Nothin New

Aint it funny how the human soul, in its cry for uniqueness and meaning, constantly comes up with stuff that's maybe specifically unique in creation, but totally generic in its type. The soul of man cries out, has always cried out, and will always cry out- for grace.

The realm of music that I am personally familiar with is rock and roll, and rhythm and blues music. I have found many, many songs by some of the world's best-known musical artists where the ache for peace, love and contentment are the theme. George Harrison's song "Give Me Love, Give me love", the Rolling Stones monster hit of the 60's, "I can't get no satisfaction", show the cry of the human soul in a life that is quite replete with the world's finest, most expensive offerings.

Lyrics in rock music come from very innovative sources, but the world's oldest lyrics in a rock song come from the book of Ecclesiastes. The song "Turn, turn, turn" by the Byrds was written as a war protest song ("a time for peace, I swear it's not too late") but popularized the Book of Ecclesiastes and its timeless wisdom.

Music is the voice of its culture. If you want to know where the good spots are, where the aches are, listen to the music. Its expression is new, its technology is new, but its message is as old as the Book of Ecclesiastes. The creation will always need its creator, and the wiser portions of it will say so.

The cry for grace in the human soul is unique and timeless, but nothin new!

Tell me what you think, I'm just thinkin out loud!

Let's go to the other side

Jesus and his disciples get to the shore, and board a boat with His admonition "let's go to the other side". So they take off across the lake. The wind is calm at first, but as they near the middle, a very threatening storm brews. Jesus is calm and secure- and asleep in the back of the boat. What was He to sweat? This trip was in His hands and it was time for a little shuteye. Meanwhile, the disciples are having their wits tested and their seaman's skills put nearly to naught. Finally, they see him still asleep in the back and wake him up with the question "Master do you not care that we are drowning?" Jesus rapped their knuckles for their lack of faith, and then commanded the sea and wind to calm down.

Now, just before they set out, didn't He say, "let us go to the other side"? So, of course this destination being His idea, He knew they were gonna make it, no matter what.

The paths in our lives are fraught with threatening storms, and they look deadly sometimes. But Jesus was still with them in the same boat- and He is still with us in ours.

Tell me what you think, I'm just thinkin out loud.

He walks through the walls!

It's easy to walk on in your life, when the problems are there, but answers are too. The verses you claim just work when you plug them in, and presto; the salvation you need is waiting to be claimed.

But when new problems come up and the solutions that used to work no longer do because circumstances are different, and the cries for help seem to fall on deaf ears, then it's time for deeper something. If all life stays at the same level of challenge, then it ceases being one. It gets boring and stale, no matter how easily we can work out a problem at that level of living. For faith to grow circumstances have to change. People have to come and go, bad things and good things need to occur to deepen our faith.

And we may resent that change, because it jars us out of our comfort zone. We shut out people, things, even God. He's no longer our lord because he changed the game or the rules of it. Deepening faith requires deepening crisis, ever harder situations to survive in. This knocks out our bad habits and tendencies and shears the sinful ways of our souls, and it hurts when it does that! Look at David's Psalms and how deadly honest he is with God. If Psalms teaches you anything it teaches you the value of honesty about your pain. It's okay to feel badly about things. It's okay not to like everything that's happening in your life. You will feel a desire to set up walls to try to lessen the pain. You're just being a human being to do that-it's called survival. Prayer gets harder to do, takes longer to express everything. But keep it up because you have got to have a place to put that pain.

As your soul grows older, your struggle grows harder and your pain goes deeper, while your faith grows stronger when you see God walk through your walls.

No matter what happens He always walks through our walls- and reassures us of His presence.

Tell me what you think, I'm just thinkin out loud!

The Only Way to do it!

Did you ever watch planes take off at an airport? The prop plane gets up to a certain speed, lifts the nose a little, and its airborne. The jets don't have it that easy. If a jet keeps its nose on the ground like that, it can't take off! It has to get up to a certain speed, lift the nose way up in the air, and then it leaves the ground.

This was discovered in wind tunnel testing way back in the late 50's, early 60's. It made takeoffs more dramatic looking, and it made flying possible with jets carrying heavy loads of fuel, luggage and people. It would seem a risky maneuver to lift the nose up like that, but when it proves itself a working process, faith in it comes easily.

In snow skiing, keeping traction on a slope when crossing it at an angle takes leaning out from the hill so the edges dig in and go forward instead of sliding sideways. The weight of the skier keeps the ski from sliding sideways as long that weight is balanced on the ski, not placed to one side. Leaning into the hill looks safe, but the skis don't work well leaning sideways. This is a clear step of faith but when it works, it happens easier with time.

The jet pilot needs faith in the process to assume that position; also the snow skier. The believer in Jesus Christ has the same situation. It takes a real step of faith to make a decision to trust, but when he does, God takes over.

Faith only works and grows one way-under pressure!

Tell me what you think, I'm just thinkin out loud!

Don't push it Away!

About noon the following day as they were on their journey and approaching the city, Peter went up on the roof to pray. He became hungry and wanted something to eat . . . heaven opened up and saw something like a large sheet being lowered to earth by its four corners. It contained all kinds of four-footed animals . . . reptiles . . . birds of the air. "Get up Peter, kill and eat!" "Surely not, Lord!," said Peter, "I have never eaten anything impure or unclean." "Do not call anything impure or unclean that the Lord has made clean".

It seems a common experience for people to turn away from something or want to, because they weren't willing to pay the price of it, even if they knew it was the right way to go. God's clear leading towards a decision is a direction toward a tough life, a life that you will need His power to execute. The only thing peaceful about it may be His blessing of knowing that you followed his will.

A new believer is like a piece of sheet metal on a roll press. That's a machine that turns flat sheet metal into those gnarly-looking pieces of siding, etc, or whatever other bent metal it's supposed to be. Sounds exciting, doesn't it! That's sanctification for ya! But you end up much more useful to God for the purposes He has for you.

You may be divorced and scared of re-marriage, because you say you don't want commitment anymore. Naaaaah! You're probably just avoiding the roll press that'll make you address the sin issues in your life that will destroy yet another marriage if they go unaddressed. That's why God, who knows what it takes to mold a soul, will do it anyway.

Sometimes the direction you are led in is not the direction you would pick. Go there anyway!

Tell me what you think, I'm just thinkin out loud!

Everybody watch what's goin down!

Revenge is so sweet! It's an irresistible delicacy. Watch Joseph, the wearer of the Technicolor Dreamcoat, as Prime Minister of Egypt. In Genesis, Chapter 42, v6 he recognizes his brothers, the progenitors of his suffering. They don't yet recognize him, and he can't resist playing a head game with them. He bats 'em around like a cat with a cornered mouse. But watch what happens later.

God uses this batting around to make them own up, fess up, and shake up. They have to be scared for their lives, a ready motivation for honesty don't you think? Joseph gets to shake these shysters down, but it comes back to bite him later on. Paul Harvey's favorite part of the story, the rest of it, happens in Chapter 45. Joseph sends all his people away, leaving him alone with his brothers- and <u>he</u> comes clean.

Galatians 6:7 has finally come true in this story: As ye sow, so shall ye also reap. The mighty man of Egypt, lord of the land, has had his day, and now it's time to pay. But Romans 8:28 is also operative here. The family moves to Egypt, lives and dies in the lap of luxury, and another chapter in Israel's history goes to the books.

When you're feelin the power, watch what you do with it- it always comes with a price!

Tell me what you think, I'm just thinkin out loud!

Why do you say that?

People sometimes tell other people " I never talk about you behind your back", and its utter nonsense! People are always discussing other people in their absence. They say good things, they say bad things, but it happens. It's not so bad that it happens either. There is a fair assessment of people happening at prayer time, at hiring time, at firing time, all the time.

What matters is the motivation of the speaker, and of the listener. Self-esteem figures in heavily, too. What motivates someone to speak ill or well is the most critical issue. Do the kind words come from a loving heart, seeking the good of the subject, or are they meant for destruction of the soul? In the latter case, the speaking soul is always the one more destroyed by the comment. People with low self-esteem are the ones blaming themselves. They will identify a sin in someone else so vividly because they carry it so well in their own hearts. But not so with a good-hearted intention motivating the comment.

Loving hearts see their previous sins in the hearts of others presently, and they pray for the person so fervently for its avoidance. If avoidance is not possible, then they want to reassure the young believer that where they are going, this person has been, step by step. This is a loving arms approach, wanting to comfort the errant one that they too, were once there.

Some people's sense of power is in their mouth, in their speech, and they use it to build up, or to tear down. Prayer gets used for sanctified gossip. Even prayer itself gets used to exalt a praying speaker to a prideful state of high self-esteem. Someone else then needs to keep a hatpin handy, to keep things under control.

But a sovereign God always reigns, and keeps those things under control. He gets the right words into the right hearts. You may not always know why something needs to be said- until later. It's really and truly fascinating!

Give your heart to God, let Him lead your words- then speak! Those are His missiles; he will aim them and make them go where he wants them to go.

Tell me what you think, I'm just thinkin out loud!

The Union of Spirits

There is a street in Memphis TN, called Union Avenue. Its name has nothing to do with the Northern Army's occupation of the city soon after the beginning of the Civil War. It is called Union Avenue because in its early days, Memphis was actually two cities, Memphis and South Memphis. Union Avenue was the common border of the two- the union of cities.

There is a context of living created by the Creator of life called marriage. It is as much a spiritual, mental and emotional state of union as it is a physical one. There are all kinds of sensations involved, and this is part of the beauty. But the marriage union is the original idea of God, the creator of all things. It is shunned and cursed by the world, eager to get a physical sensation from the glorifying of the physical beyond its place. The violation of a design doesn't invalidate the design or weaken it necessarily. Instead its strength shows through, because it is a valid, workable, durable concept to begin with.

The design of marriage is first spiritual, then emotional, mental and finally physical. The last three don't give as good results unless the first is observed. "The union of your spirits here has caused Him to remain, for whenever two or more of you are gathered in His Name, there is love". Paul Stookey hit it right on the head!

Bring first spirits together then heads, hearts and then bodies, in the fashion intended by the Creator of us all, and then the union of these gets as good as it can possibly get!

Tell me what you think, I'm just thinkin out loud!

Meet Dave in the Cave

A man driving a car had a blowout while on the highway. Although it dazed him at first, he was alert enough to get himself and his car out of harm's way. He got out and pulled out the tire tools, a spare tire and went to work changing tires. He couldn't lift the corner of the car, at least not high enough to free the damaged tire, so he put the jack in place and turned the wheel so the jack lifted the car. Lacking sufficient physical strength, he went to a resource at hand to do the job for him- the jack. It did the heavy lifting he couldn't do by himself.

Young David in the Old Testament gave us a book full of words he spoke when life's situations overwhelmed him-Psalms. He mentioned his pursuers, his frustrations with them and with God for not saving him on his own timetable. He also poured out praise for all the times he knew God had saved him from his enemies, his fears, his frustrations, etc. He said a lot of this in a cave, a place he knew he could go and hide and pour out his heart without stopping. Probably took him all night to do that because pain doesn't find the exit door very quickly sometimes. When you are hurting very badly, it can be a long time before peace comes. But come it does-in His time.

Sometimes prayer is all you have for dealing with life-that's when it's all you need!

Tell me what you think, I'm just thinkin out loud!

Don't look at the odds, look at your God!

What a chicken that Gideon started out to be in Judges, Chapter 6! A more contemporary paraphrase of his first answer might read- The Lord is with us, RIGHT! Then explain why this Lord has the Midianites beating us to a pulp constantly. God understood his confusion here, and dismissed his complaint, saying "Go in the strength you have, and save Israel out of the hand of the Midianites." Gideon put this message to a test, to see if it really was from God. Once he got that part straight, he went to work. First he smashed the altar of Baal, and built an altar to God to show which God he belonged to. But the next part is even gutsier- he went to war against an army too large to count with only 300 men, armed with clay jars and trumpets! Gideon didn't look at his odds, he looked at His God!

Tight as a drum is an apt description of Jericho in the days before its walls fell. Joshua 6 says-Now Jericho was tightly shut up because of the Israelites; no one went out and no one came in. But Joshua and his army had no trouble entering when it was time. He had his marching army circle the city with the priests carrying trumpets of ram's horns, which they played as they marched around the city, once a day for 6 days. On the seventh day, they marched around Jericho seven times, and then gave a long honk on the horns, followed by a shout- and the walls came a tumblin down. Joshua had fought many a battle in the strength of his God before that, but this still took some looking at his God to pull off. He didn't look at his odds, he looked at his God!

When we face the enemy, the circumstances, the hearts of people, don't we always have some doubt about the outcome? Isn't it reasonable to fear failure, even though we know God is on our side? But we always have to give up our fear when we know it is His will that leads what we do. We have to take our eyes off our odds- the negatives we face- and look at our God.

Don't look at the odds, look at your God, because it's always His fight!

Tell me what you think, I'm just thinkin out loud!

Someone to take out the tangles

My friend needed someone who had a brush and a will strong enough to brush out her long hair. I loved doing this as she has beautiful hair, and it helps everyone else who sees her to notice that beauty that I see in her. When I can brush out her tangles it gives her hair a shine that can't come through with the tangles underneath. She says she can feel those tangles, and so appreciates me pulling them out.

Seems like life and how we respond to it creates tangles in our souls, and we need friends willing to cause the pain we might have when they address our tangles and help us get them out. We need to be willing to put up with pain here and there. This way they can smooth things out and have us looking and being as good as we can.

What do you say to high school friends who go out and get drunk with their buddies leaving no one sober to drive the car and avoid an accident? Who's got a friend there? It takes someone with character to stand up and prevent someone else from hurting themselves. What's a friend for when you can't count on them to save you from yourself sometimes?

It's not good grooming to ignore the tangles in your hair. Its not good friendship for someone else to ignore the tangles in your life, and not at least offer to help with them.

Tell me what you think, I'm just thinking out loud!

Do it Anyway

She loved him. He grew to love her, despite warning signs against the idea. This time he didn't see the signs anymore, and he felt the peace of God telling him to go ahead, be involved with her, love her, marry her, and stay with her as best he could. He did.

This was something human wisdom would have had all kinds of problems with. The red flags were there; the signs of warning were there. Weren't they there for Gideon when he went to battle with 300 soldiers against an uncountable enemy? Weren't they there when Joshua walked around Jericho with a brass section to take down a wall? When someone else went to war with the jawbone of a donkey, wasn't it at least humanly questionable how it might turn out?

When God is there, that's all it takes to win. When he says do it, and you do, that's all you need. Though it takes a turn for the worse, though it looks absolutely hopeless, hang on, certain that you did what God said do. He opened a door, you went through it. He showed you direction and made promises in the light. Keep that certainty and those promises in your heart.

Never doubt in the darkness what God has shown you in the light!

Tell me what you think, I'm just thinkin out loud.

Keep a Good Eye!

The pitcher winds up and throws a screaming curveball toward home plate. The batter sees it coming, and instead of a swing, he gives it a mean look and backs up to dodge it. The ump says "Ball 1".

A voice comes out of the dugout "good eye!". A photographer wins an award for a photograph, and all who look and admire the photo also admire the photographer for having a "good eye".

What is this good eye? A sphere in the head delivering visual information to the brain, or also a sphere in the head guided by the brain's experiences that confirms the wisdom of the proper athletic move or better way to look at a sight?

Romans 12:3 tells us not to think of ourselves too highly but to think so as to have sound judgment. What is this sound judgment? Is it not a realistic assessment of gifts, abilities, and other attributes of a person as they see themselves? What kinds of things affect this? Sin surely does, since it causes one to judge oneself more harshly than is right, coming from self-judgment as it does. But an ingestion of harmful substances or lack of necessary ingestion of beneficial ones can also do this, to body and mind. Both interfere with keeping a "good eye", and neither has a place in a person's life, no matter what the feeling is that is gained. It's really not a gain, just a sensation, like an incorrect gauge reading on a dial. It gives the wrong information, and can lead to wrong decisions.

So don't go feeling haughty or horrible about yourself-keep a good eye!

Tell me what you think, I'm just thinkin out loud!

Growing through the Good Hurts

It's amazing what people think they can do with relatively little experience in a given area. I've heard one politician say he thought he knew how to legislate- until he got elected, and spent a year learning how to do his job effectively.

So many believers think they have their lives together and with Scripture they have God by the tail. Just claim a verse here, cite a passage there, and life is their oyster. Then they get to growing, emotionally, spiritually, mentally, physically- and they start learning how to live. After Joni Eareckson had her infamous dive, which paralyzed her greatly, she and a boyfriend thought they could just plug in a verse and she would be healed. It really caused them some hard thinking when she had to stay in the chair. It's the hurts we don't expect that really knock us down. It wasn't supposed to go this way or that- but it did. Recovering from those hurts is where we get a better sense of ourselves, and what we can or cannot do, or should not try.

Passion is a great and terrible emotional drive. It moves without reason sometimes. We get into something and sometimes get hurt. But we come away with a greater sense of control of that drive. We move with more discernment the next time because of the terrible bruising we took the last time we let ourselves go. That's what makes the pain a good hurt- it helped us grow in mind and heart. But it takes remembering the lessons-history unheeded gets repeated!

Life is a hard process- very doable, but we only grow if we learn from its lessons! It's what growing through the good hurts is about.

Tell me what you think, I'm just thinkin out loud.

Getting to Jericho

Joshua fit the battle of Jericho, Jericho, Jericho
Joshua fit the battle of Jericho,
And the walls came tumblin down

Riiiiight up to the walls of Jericho, he
marched with spear in hand
Ole Joshua commanded those children to shout!
Cause the battle am in my hand

Neat little story, huh? Joshua marches his army around a city for several days, then several times around on one day, cuts loose with a horn section- and down come some layers of protection that surrounded a city, made it feel safe. Then in went the warriors to defeat the enemy within.

Nice little paradigm for God's warriors, actually. There was repeated obedience; a practiced approach- and the defenses melted away. Worked with a city, works with people. Jericho is geographically a city, a collection of people with evil intent. Conceptually Jericho is one person with an impenetrable wall of defense, dealing with the world from behind that wall. Inside is any number of demonically inspired ways of protecting themselves. It takes spiritual tools to deal with them.

But notice Joshua. He says, "the battle am in my hand". What confidence! What steadfast attitude that with obedience and the means to deal with the opposition within, this is a done deal. Joshua had his role down, and he had God's role down. Approach, speak to the issue, and let God do the rest. There was what Joshua knew what he could do, what only God could do, and it made a winning plan.

Music theorists have long wondered what natural phenomenon could have taken part to make a very thick brick wall come down at the sound of horns. The world cannot allow a miracle; it's just too out of their minds. Miracles don't belong in our heads, they belong in our hearts. That's where faith is, because it lies out of the realm of our possibility.

It always takes a miracle to get to Jericho.

Tell me what you think, I'm just thinkin out loud!

Unrepayable Grace
Matthew 18:21-35

Amount Owed 10000 talents
In Gold coin

12/13/2012 $ 1,697.60   per ounce

1 talent = 75 lbs.
1 lb.= 16 ounces

    10000   75   750000
    750000   16   12000000
    12000000 $ 1,697.60

$20,371,200,000.00!!!

What COULD a servant do to rack up that much debt? What do WE do?

John 3:16 is about MUCH greater debt than this. What have you done about that?

The 4:6 Fix

Humpty Dumpty sat on a wall,
Humpty Dumpty had a great fall!
All the king's horses, and all the king's men
Couldn't put Humpty back together again.

Poor guy, once a proud egg, perched on a wall, then a big

gooooey mess of yolk, white mixed in with shards of shell. Oooooooooooooooooooh! Yuck!

Who wants to try to fix that one? Who can? Doesn't matter whether he was pushed or not, he's history as an egg. Situations like his, while obviously something the king's horses, or their men can't fix, aren't always so obvious that we can't. Caused or not, it happened.

Here we are, with the big messes, the impossible circumstances in our lives, and we strain to come up with a solution. Such situations aren't subject to our solving, not in the least. It causes a HUGE amount of anxiety, sleeplessness, because under normal circumstances we can, and we should try.

Enter Zechariah 4:6: *Not by power, not by might, but by My Spirit, saith the Lord of Hosts.* There will be situations that arise in our lives, that will seem fixable in our power, but they really aren't. God is the one we have to rely on to carry us through, and take care of ALL the details. It will prove quite impossible for us to do anything but pray over them. It's the 4:6 fix.

Tis such an affront to human pride, but that is precisely the point. It's way off the end of ourselves, way past our ability. Its Dave in the Cave stuff, where the only appropriate position is on our knees, acknowledging our need of a Saviour. That's just not always obvious to us, though.

Some situations need a 4:6 fix.

Tell me what you think, I'm just thinkin out loud.

Let Him out!

A divine Creator created a creation that is losing its mind by trying to contain the Creator! Here he is, large beyond any creative thought, yet the creature won't let Him be himself!

We humans come up with our business plans, and attempt to design plans of action that are good and sensible courses of action for PEOPLE to follow. Where we err is in expecting God to **always** go with our ideas of how to accomplish His work.

The only part of the Almighty God that is designed to stay inside of a human is that His Spirit is designed to be inside of our spirit, and that is it! Any other kind of containment on our part is not good. We may have his heart to some respect, but even that can limit Him, because the biggest fallacy of humanity is this notion that His mind will stay within our bounds of logic.

When God calls someone to His service, he is inside the mind just enough to get them to see what He wants them to do. Once He has that mind firmly hooked on that concept, he takes off. Once He has us in tow, it is only our part to let Him go! God tells the servant three things:

1) This is what I want you to do
2) Maintenance of your life's needs is MY problem
3) DON'T tell ME how to do that!

The wild and hairy adventure of obeying a known leading will get needlessly scary and painful when the called believer doesn't let the Creator take him through the adventure of growth by <u>His</u> means. Conventional wisdom is something God will use in some ways, but something He will toss aside in others. There will be pain to teach character, poverty to teach contentment and wild stretching to teach a believer how to trust Him to provide for needs without constraining His ways to human logical limits.

I know of a belief system that contains God to concepts. He is a person, not a concept, leading me to say that worship of a concept is NOT his idea of true worship. No wonder that group is struggling. They are not meeting the truly human needs of the human soul to worship God as they were created to.

While we have a grasp of His thoughts and ways, we never have containment!

Tell me what you think, I'm just thinkin out loud!

Shifting Gears in Midstream

When a 50-something couple found themselves called to the mission field, it was a classic clash of the titans: God of the Universe meets the value system of the Baby Boomers. He's thinking, "Lets get this bunch of folks out on the mission field where I want them". They're thinking normal Baby Boomer thoughts, like what about the IRA? The 401k, and getting geared down for retirement in a few years?

He made it clear to them separately what HE wanted them to do, and they had to decide just WHO really was #1 in their lives, and how should they respond to a call to do something they really didn't want to do. Guess who won that one?

Add to this the thought of raising support to answer the call to go in a recession economy. It's the kind of stuff to put you on your face in prayer and keep it there until things are clearer. Thoughts arise like "who's in charge here?" and who's responsible for maintenance after all?

Old Testament battles with weapons like jawbones, brass sections, and vastly outnumbered armies clanging noisemakers on the offensive go 21st Century real quick, because it's precisely the same type of battle, calling for the same level of faith. It's even the same question- just WHO is Lord? Both types of warriors get the exact same answer- their God.

What's YOUR battle? Who's YOUR GOD? Figure out those two, and the situation becomes clearer what to do about it.

Tell me what you think, I'm just thinkin out loud!

A Sovereignty of Purpose

In Exodus, God has brought His people to Egypt to preserve them through some very hard times. He does that with His own. They still come to know leanness of spirit in the hard times, but it serves its purpose in driving them closer to Him. What did God tell Moses when He called him to lead the children of Israel out of Egypt- "I have indeed seen the misery of my people in Egypt . . ." The Jews wailed long and loud, finally breaking down and crying out to their God, and He answered.

Where was Moses when he heard this? In Midian. How'd he end up there? Wasn't he the son of Pharaoh's daughter? Wasn't he a "castle kid", growing up in the luxury of the king? Yes, but Moses was Moses, and his reaction to a situation landed him in Midian. Moses's own personality, his conviction as a Hebrew, and his passion about it, led him to expose his Jewishness and to his flight.

People's passion about issues, our intense desire to right wrongs, to administer justice, is often misdirected, but always under sovereign control. God always takes us as we are, and uses the way He made us, to effect His purposes. What if Moses had left that situation alone, and continued living in Pharaoh's house? Would he not have possibly met and married an Egyptian woman and so intermingled Israel's blood with Egypt's? His passion about his people led to a rash act, which signalled a plot turn that kept his people pure and distinct in Egyptian society.

So, the plan of God to keep His people separate from their surroundings works out in the very biological, emotional, and psychological being that Moses was, and we are. He might not have ended up shepherding in Midian, if he hadn't been a passionate Jew in Egypt. Who he was took him where he was, in Midian. There's where he found out about his Lord's plan for the rest of his life.

God's plan shows us where to go, and His sovereignty gets us there.

Tell me what you think, I'm just thinkin out loud!

Mustangs and belly buttons

It was late in the spring of 1964 when Ford Motor Co. introduced a mid-season entry in the car market that captured the American fantasy like nothing before its time. The Mustang was an immediate favorite with all classes of car buyers, and became visible nearly everywhere you looked. By four years later, it was said that Mustangs were like belly buttons-everybody had one!

The human concept of self-esteem is exactly like that. Everybody has one. Some people's esteem is high, some is low, but every human being has an opinion of himself or herself, and it shows in everything they do. Choices on every level reflect how a person sees their self in the world. Sometimes clothing or other visible choices reflect how they want to feel about themselves. That's the "fake it till ya make it" idea. Sometimes the self-image needs burnishing, and a new dress or hair style will do it for a woman, or a fancy car will do it for a man.

Self-esteem most visibly makes its mark in friends. People have in their lives the people they either want or feel they deserve. Every friend you have either shows how you feel about yourself, or want to. They way they treat you shows how you see yourself, because you have in your soul a person who deserves or wants to be either loved or hated. It makes us take on people who fascinate us, and mistreat us. Takes a lot of digging to find out what's driving our desires and choices. But it's a worthwhile effort, this venture, because it can show us our unhealthy choices, the ones that eminently lead to our destruction. A skilled person can show us how to face them, realize what's driving them, and stop making them.

We're not always so pretty inside, but God's grace can clean that up. He begins by taking away the sin load, the feeling that we should trash ourselves, because of previous choices and actions. Once that burden is off of us, we can then start loving ourselves, and making decisions that reflect that love.

A work of grace is a life of ever healthier choices, leading to ever better self esteem. It makes for a sound mind, as well.

Tell me what you think, I'm just thinkin out loud.

Between glancing and looking

In the busy-ness of life in this day and age, glancing comes easy, and looking takes effort, so most things get a glance, and not near enough other things get a real look. When you glance you look at something and take in maybe one detail, whereas you study something in a look. You get lots more useful-actually critical-information.

This leaves you with a different reaction than maybe you should have. A glance at the object on your periphery in the street tells you its an object, the look tells you it's a kid, on a bike, and he may not see you coming ahead. The result can be the difference between a stop, and an unfortunate accident.

Look at Psalm 46:10- Be still, and know that I am God. Here, you're seeing a command that says WAY more than stop your motion! The kid in the seat moves about, and you tell them "be still", so their movement does not create a disturbance. But this "be still" is not really about the lack of motion. Its about regarding life, having, or exercising control in a situation. Back off, make no effort at control or even influence past prayer, and let the Divine One take over.

Next we see "and know that I am God". Here's where you not only back off the exercise of effort, but know that the one you are handing it off to is

MORE than able to take care of it. What peace we can have from knowing and acknowledging His almighty Lordship of EVERYthing! Get your hands off, and let Him handle it-Be Still.

Tell me what you think, I'm just thinkin out loud!

Like bumps on the ground

I once took a plane ride from Denver CO to Ontario CA. It was a very eye opening ride, as the climb to cruise altitude gave me a unique perspective on the Rocky Mountains. Once you climb high enough, those mountains that look so imposing from a car on I-70 in the middle of them, end up looking like bumps on the ground.

People who grow in their faith do so because they lift ever harder prayer requests and they see ever greater answers. The history of the answers gives one the confidence that the issues facing believers are just some more mountains to climb in faith. But aren't we ever smaller ants in the face of the mountains we face? Looking thru a prayer list is like driving among the highest peaks in the Rocky Mountains.

But the act of prayer puts our issues in the hands of the maker of the mountains. We get elevated to high flying altitudes when we lift up the problems because we assume the perspective of the one we hand them to.

Philippians 4:7 helps out with this because it addresses the stress associated with the problem. Once the pain is lifted, our spirits soar, and the mountains we feared and felt intimidated by end up looking like bumps on the ground. This all takes time to do. A lot of time has to pass, and the mountains change from the Rockies to the Himalayas! But we <u>still</u> fly over em.

Tell me what you think, I'm just thinkin out loud!

The Mechanics of Ministry

To understand what goes on when a spiritual activity such as ministering takes place, it is best to first back away and explain the process of communication between one individual and another, or others. Simply put, communication occurs when one person speaks words to another, and that person hears and understands the words, so that the intended thought goes completely, successfully from one mind to the other.

What is happening in ministry is a bit more complicated. To properly and correctly convey a spiritual thought, it needs understanding that the thought itself begins with God. He puts the thought into the mind of the person speaking, and that person speaks the appropriate words to correctly convey the thought to the listener. This is where God the Holy Spirit comes into the process. The thought, being from the Father, needs the personal experience of the speaker and the conveyance of conviction within the heart of the hearer, to fully complete the process. It is this combination of experience and conviction that not only impresses the force of the thought, but also the ability to understand the thought, because it is not only the particular words that do the job. Words are mechanical creations, made by the mechanical motion of speech. The thought, the particular intention of understanding, is made possible only as the Spirit has been able to so permeate the soul, heart and life of the person speaking, that the Spirit works through the very words spoken. Paul spoke like a high-speaking, learned man of his day. Peter was said to be more the street talker. God used both men to convey His thoughts and feelings to the audiences that each of these people spoke to. So, while there is Divine origination of thought, there is individual expression of it by the person speaking. In each case, Divine thought and conviction are expressed, received and understood.

But, while communication may be happening, reception may be meeting with resistance in the heart of the hearer. People still have a will. People can harden their hearts. Some will disagree with this idea, but there is the verse in the Old Testament "do not harden your hearts" (Ps. 95:8, Heb 3:8)

And, another factor which figures in is the heart of the speaker. If that person is not given to being available to God for Him to work in his own heart, then how can the speaker speak spiritual truth and know that he is truly ministering? Some preachers can speak for hours, and their words fall on the floor, never getting inside a soul. Prayer and seeking the Giver of the Message are the prerequisites of the speaker before he EVER dares to speak a word of prophecy!

These mechanics of ministry particularly come into play in the act of comforting. People often visit grieving people and say the exact wrong words! Or they say what are appropriate words, but no comforting happens. The Holy Spirit is doing the comforting, to be sure. People can just show up, and be there, and the very presence is used in the heart of the one grieving to comfort them.

Words go to the ears; comfort and conviction go to the heart. That's the mechanics of ministry! The speaker speaks to the part outside, the ears, and the Holy Spirit works to the part inside, the heart, and that makes it happen!

Tell me what you think, I'm just thinkin out loud!

Did you ever go through an experience and wonder what the lesson was, learn that, and want to share it, so someone else might benefit from your reaction? Not that everybody was going to have the same reaction, but some would. Everybody has an audience on nearly every lesson they learn. So goes it for what's in this book. You'll really pick up some wisdom, ignore the rest. It's all an individual reaction. Still there's enough lessons learned by me to help somebody, maybe even several somebodies. What made this book get written was one reaction two years out of college and another one several years later. The first was a hug from a guy who had listened to me week after week, sharing what I'd learned lately at a fellowship. He saw me that night, at a restaurant, and gave me a big hug, and said what I'd shared had blessed him. Funny, no one ever shared that they were being blessed during the time when I was sharing them. Still, the leaders of the fellowship must have felt led to leave me alone, and let the Spirit lead in the sharing. Another encouragement came from my senior minister at the time, Dr. John R. de Witt. Dr. de Witt had read some of my writing, in one form or another, and was apparently impressed. Here was a former seminary professor, author of numerous books, and he was encouraging ME?! He called it my best gift! WOW! That was the final push that I needed to begin writing on whatever topic I felt inspired to write. It all really amounts to a travelogue of spiritual growth over time. But I know it's bound to help somebody, sometime, so here it is!